Rolf Harris
on Safari
Quiz Book

Look-in Books

Jointly published by
INDEPENDENT TELEVISION BOOKS LTD
247 Tottenham Court Road, London W1P 0AU

and

ARROW BOOKS LTD
3 Fitzroy Square, London W1

An imprint of the Hutchinson Publishing Group

London Melbourne Sydney Auckland Wellington Johannesburg and agencies throughout the world

First published 1979
© Martin Banks 1979

Photoset in Times Medium 10/11 pt
by Yale Press, Norwood

Cover photograph Ron McFarlane and E.P.L.

ISBN: 0 09 919660 3

CONDITIONS OF SALE:
This book shall not, by way of trade or otherwise, be lent, re-sold, hired out or otherwise circulated without the publisher's prior consent in any form of binding or cover other than that in which it is published and without a similar condition including this condition being imposed on the subsequent purchaser.

Printed in Great Britain by
Hazell Watson & Viney Ltd, Aylesbury, Bucks

Rolf Harris
on Safari
Quiz Book

Martin Banks

Illustrated by
Susan Neale

Look-in Books

Contents

Foreword by Rolf Harris — 5

Introduction — 6

Whales, dolphins, seals, sea lions, walruses and sea cows — 9

Elephants, rhinoceroses, hippopotami and tapirs — 21

Horses, asses and zebras — 38

Antelope, deer, cattle, giraffes and okapi — 52

Camels and llamas, wild goats, sheep and pigs — 69

The big cats — 86

Bears, wolves and wild dogs — 101

Apes, monkeys and lemurs — 114

Foreword

For many years now I have been concerned for the well being and protection of all animals, large or small. It is a pleasure therefore to join up with Martin Banks in a quiz book about our nearest animal neighbours... that is the mammals. After all man himself is a mammal, isn't he?

Martin is as concerned as myself that mankind treats the animal world with respect and that species in danger of extinction are protected and preserved for the future.

Like most things in life, once you get to know a bit more about something or someone, then you start to feel a little more friendly towards them. Well, in this book there are hundreds and hundreds of interesting facts and snippets that will clear up some of the myths and questions all of us have asked about the larger of our animal neighbours, from whales to lions, apes to camels, buffaloes to zebras.

Furthermore you don't have to be a white-hunter or international traveller to see many of the mammals covered here — just go to your local zoo or wildlife park and have a good look.

Happy reading then...

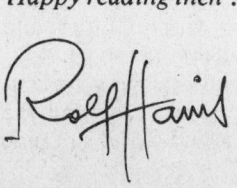

Introduction

Almost everybody knows what a lion looks like. Or a tiger, or an elephant. Although they may never have lived wild in our own part of the world (or not since prehistoric times), we can see live specimens of these and many other animals in our zoos, circuses and wildlife parks. In illustrated books, in museums and on the television screen we can see what almost any animal looks like that has ever existed — from long-lost mammoths and dodos to the rarest wild animals that still exist today.

It is very important that we should have a better understanding of the animals which still share our world. Many of them are threatened with extinction, which means that there is a grave danger that they will die out completely unless something is done to save them. Many have already disappeared long ago, through hunting or changes in the climate, and if we are not careful we could lose the rest.

The huge dinosaurs which roamed the earth millions of years ago vanished because they were unable to evolve or adapt enough to the changes in climate and temperature which gradually altered their world. Nowadays the cause of an animal's extinction is much more likely to be man. We have moved in on the wild places of the earth and spoiled them with our cities: and we have hunted the animals for food and for sport.

All over the world we have been destroying forests, digging up grasslands, polluting rivers, upsetting the balance of the seas and even interfering with the desert.

Despite all this destruction a great variety of animals still manage to survive, and, fortunately, we now seem to have begun to come to our senses, although not a minute too soon. Trained scientists who know about plants and animals and the effect man has on them, and who know how vital the natural world is to our own survival, have persuaded us to watch what we are doing. In many parts of the world, wildlife is now protected in reserves and national parks. Even outside these areas hunting may be strictly controlled.

Until quite recently, a great deal of what we knew about animals was passed on to us by hunters and explorers, or was the product of folklore and myth. The only animals that were examined closely were dead ones, and the only animals whose behaviour was studied at all, were those living very unnatural lives in captivity. Now more and more people are becoming involved in the study of how animals live and behave, and much of the earlier information has been shown to be untrue in the light of more recent and more accurate observations.

The study of how animals behave is known as ethology, and it is very important for at least two reasons. Firstly, knowing exactly how animals live and behave gives us a better idea of how to conserve them. Secondly, since we are also animals, the more we know about our fellow animals the more we can learn about ourselves.

Although new facts about animals are discovered every day, there is still a lot to learn. Even if it isn't possible for us to go to all the places in the world where animals live naturally, we can still learn a great deal by watching animals in good zoos and wildlife parks, where they behave very much like their wild relatives. Patience and accurate observation will sometimes reveal things which have never been noticed before! Much of what we know about the way animals behave is the result of years of scientific research, but a chance observation has often completely changed what we thought we knew.

Binoculars can be useful for studying animal behaviour. In the wide open spaces of Africa, for example, they are almost essential. But animals in captivity are very easy to study without such aids. All you need is your eyes and a lot of time and patience — and perhaps a notebook. One useful tip is that most animals (including those in the wild) are more active during the early morning and the evening than in the middle of the day. And a visit to a zoo or wildlife park on a cold winter's day may be far more rewarding than you think it's going to be, because many species are much more lively then than in hot summer weather.

What are mammals?

Mammals are all those animals which are warm-blooded, have a covering of hair and give birth to live young which are suckled on milk produced by the mother. Perhaps the best-known mammal of all is Man.

There are over 4000 different species of mammal alive today. Scientists group them into 19 different scientific *orders:* each order contains several different *families,* and each family is made up of mammals which are more like each other than they are like any of the other families. In each family there are a number different *species:* for example, the gorilla, the orangutan and the chimpanzee are all *species* of ape, which is one of the *families* in the *order* of primates (which includes us!). In this book are just some of the things we know about the larger mammals of the world. Perhaps you will be able to add to them in the future.

Martin Banks

Whales, dolphins, seals, sea lions, walruses and sea cows

The creatures in this chapter share a common home, the sea. They have all developed a way of life which allows them to spend most, or even all, of their time in the water. The whales and dolphins show the most outstanding adaptations: like all mammals they breathe air, but they are also equipped for a life spent entirely in the water, even when producing their young. Their bodies are superbly streamlined for moving through water; their front 'legs' are powerful flippers, and instead of hind legs they have powerful fins and 'fluked' (or forked) tails. Seals and sea lions come ashore to rest and breed, but they too are marvellously adapted for a life spent chiefly swimming, and they find it difficult to move about on land. Sea cows are curious creatures which feed on vegetation in rivers and shallow seas (there are two sorts, manatees and dugongs).

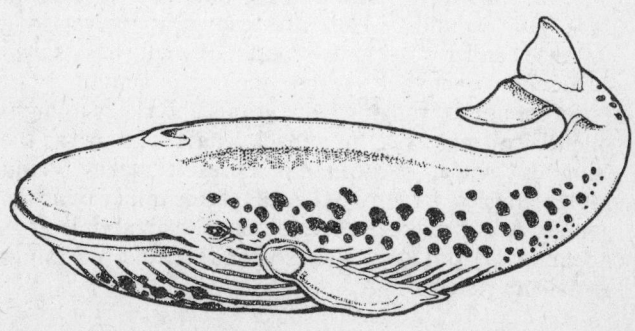

Blue whale

Which is the largest species of whale?

The blue whale is the largest of all the whales — indeed, the largest of all mammals, living today. Adult blue whales may reach a total length of over 30.5 metres (approximately 100 feet). This species is now very rare, but if you want to see what it looks like, there is a reconstructed model of a blue whale in the Natural History Museum in South Kensington, London.

How do whales feed?

Whales are divided into two main types, toothed whales and baleen whales. Toothed whales feed on fish. Baleen whales feed almost entirely on krill (tiny shrimps which are found in great concentrations in the sea). Baleen whales are so-called because they have a sieve-like structure, called a 'baleen', attached to their upper jaws. In order to feed on krill, these whales take vast quantities of water into their huge mouths, and then strain it out through the baleen filters and swallow the krill.

How do whales communicate?

Nobody yet knows exactly how whales communicate. They do not have vocal chords, but they do make a variety of sounds which are known to travel long distances under water. Each species of whale has its own particular 'language' consisting of a number of different noises, ranging from grunts and clicks to high-pitched squeaks. The humpback whale is known as the 'singing' whale, because the noises it makes sound rather musical. Many scientists now think that the sounds whales make may represent a language at least as advanced as our own. But so far the exact meanings remain a mystery.

Why are many species of whale now so rare?

Nearly all the species of larger whale have suffered from over-hunting. Commercial whaling in the past was responsible for the death of large numbers of whales, with the result that today several species are on the verge of extinction. Whales were hunted for their fat, which is known as 'blubber'. Products made from whale blubber include oil, perfumes and pet foods. Nowadays, all of these can be produced from other sources. Many countries have now agreed to cease whaling operations altogether.

Where do whales breed?

Most species use warm, shallow seas for breeding. Some whales go to the same place each year. These areas are often close to shore, in secluded bays away from disturbance and ocean storms. The whales often travel thousands of miles from their feeding grounds, out in the oceans, to the areas where they will mate and give birth, returning to the open sea later.

How long is it before a baby whale is born?

This varies according to the species of whale and its relative size, but the average is 12 months. Most female whales are believed to mate in the breeding areas one year, and give birth on their return the following year. At birth, the young whale is helped to the surface so that it may breathe. The young whale travels with its mother and suckles from her for many months.

Are whales dangerous?

The sheer size of a whale means that it is potentially a dangerous animal. There are many stories and legends that tell of whales destroying the early whaling ships and killing their crews. But in nearly all cases the men involved were hunting and harpooning whales and the animals were either wounded or defending their young. It is now known that whales are among the most good-tempered and least aggressive of all mammals, despite their great size. The grampus or killer whale has a reputation for being particularly unpredictable and dangerous. It is, for example, a voracious killer of seals and penguins. But members of this species have been tamed and trained in captivity, where they show a remarkably calm disposition and a ready willingness to co-operate with their trainers.

How do dolphins and porpoises differ from whales?

Dolphins and porpoises are in fact small, toothed whales, and like all whales belong to the order *Cetacea*. They feed on fish. While all the larger whales live in the sea, some species of dolphin live in fresh water, in large rivers or river estuaries. They are streamlined for life in the water and, like other whales, appear friendly and intelligent.

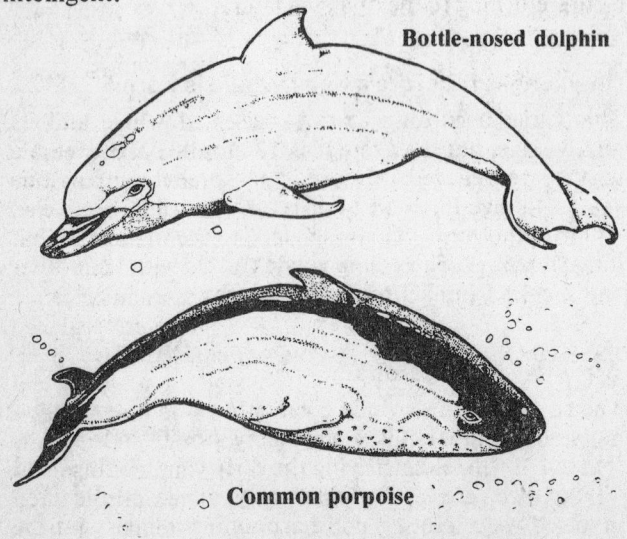

Bottle-nosed dolphin

Common porpoise

Are dolphins more intelligent than whales?

Not really. Some scientists believe that dolphins possess an intelligence equal to our own, but this may also be true of the larger whales. Because they are smaller, dolphins are quicker off the mark, and easier to study, than the big whales. They react to training with apparent enjoyment, and some have been trained to carry out quite complicated orders and movements.

Are whales and dolphins ever seen in the seas around Britain?

Most species of whale live in the vast expanses of the open seas and only come inshore to breed in tropical latitudes. But individuals do frequently appear in British waters. They sometimes become stranded on our beaches, or lose their way and swim into shallow bays or river estuaries. When this happens, the whale is often sick or has become bewildered. But some of the smaller whales do come past our shores deliberately in the course of their travels.

Dolphins usually live in tropical seas, but they too may occasionally appear close to shore around Britain. In several cases individual dolphins have taken up temporary residence for several weeks or even months along one stretch of coast. If this happens to be near a seaside town or resort, the dolphin may become quite tame and playful with swimmers. In such cases they often disappear at the end of the summer when the holiday swimmers have gone home.

One species, the common porpoise, lives in the north Atlantic. Groups (or 'schools') of these creatures are not an uncommon sight around our coasts.

Can whales and dolphins live out of the water?

Only for short periods of time. The skin of a whale or dolphin is very sensitive and soon becomes dried out if it loses contact with the water for any length of time.

Although whales and dolphins breathe air, a beached animal will die if it is not returned to the water within a short time. Even if the skin is not burnt or cracked by the sun, there is still a danger that the animal's internal organs will be damaged because of the great weight of its body pressing down on them. In the water, this weight is supported and held away from the inner organs.

Performing whales and dolphins are sometimes transported from one country to another by air. When this is done, the animal's body is supported in a specially designed sling-cradle, and its skin is kept supple by regular showers of water. In this way the animal can last a number of hours out of water without harm.

What is a narwhal?

The narwhal is one of the smaller toothed whales. It has teeth only in the upper jaw, and in adult males one of the front incisor teeth grows extra long. This single tooth may reach a metre in length! Just occasionally, a male narwhal may grow two such tusks, but normally only the left-hand incisor develops in this fashion. This tusk (which is a spiral shape) may be responsible for the legendary tales of the unicorn.

What is the difference between a seal and a sea lion?

Both belong to the order *Pinnipedia,* but sea lions form one family and seals another. Seals are heavier and more sluggish creatures than sea lions, although they are still beautifully streamlined when swimming. The more agile and lightly built sea lions are able to put their hind flippers under their bodies and use them as feet on dry land. Seals (which only come ashore to breed and moult) can only shuffle around by pulling themselves along with their fore-flippers, which are less well

developed than those of the sea lion. Sea lions also have external ears, which seals do not.

Where do sea lions live?

Sea lions are found in both the northern and southern hemispheres, living off the coasts of the continents of North and South America and Asia. They are also found around the coasts of several groups of oceanic islands, such as the Galapagos Islands in the Pacific Ocean. Several different species exist, those in colder regions being more heavily furred than those which live in the warmer seas.

Where do the sea lions in zoos and circuses come from?

Several species of sea lion are kept successfully in zoos, but the most commonly kept species, and almost the only one used in circuses, is the Californian sea lion, which inhabits the Pacific coast of North America.

Do sea lions need water in which to live?

Since sea lions (like seals) spend a great deal of their time in water, that is where they are most at home. But they can move quite fast on land. When completely dry, they lose their sleek, shiny appearance and turn a yellowish brown, the natural colour of their fur. They *can* be kept without water to swim in, but this is as unnatural to them as it would be for us to have to live in water all the time.

What do seals and sea lions eat?

Seals and sea lions normally exist on a diet of fresh fish, which they catch underwater where they can move at an amazing speed. You have probably seen sea lions at the zoo 'torpedoing' through the water at great speed after fish that the keeper throws to them.

What are the correct names for male, female and young seals?

Male seals and sea lions are called 'bulls'. The females are 'cows' and the young, 'pups'. When seals and sea lions come ashore to breed, they gather in large numbers called 'rookeries'. Each adult bull gathers a harem of females around him, and then attempts to defend them from other bulls. A sea lion rookery is in a continual state of unrest, with lots of noise and squabbling.

Which is the rarest of the seals?

Probably the Caribbean monk seal. But since no one can absolutely prove that he has seen one recently the species may actually be extinct by now. Two other species of monk seal also exist, in the Mediterranean and in the waters around Hawaii. Both are in danger of extinction since there are very few remote and undisturbed beaches left where they can breed.

What are the chief enemies of seals and sea lions?

Seals and sea lions have relatively few natural enemies, but those living in Arctic regions are preyed on by polar bears, and killer whales will certainly eat any unlucky seal they catch. Man is also an enemy. In the past, he killed off large numbers of fur-bearing sea lions, known as fur seals. Eskimos hunt the northern seals for their meat and hides, but not in sufficient numbers to reduce the population in a big way. However large numbers of young seals are killed today not only for their coats but also because seals are thought to compete with man for the fish in the sea. Such organized and artificial control of an animal's numbers is known as 'culling'. In the case of seals culling has caused a lot of argument.

Which is the largest of the seals?

The elephant seal. The bulls (which in all species of seal and sea lion are larger than the cows) may measure over 6.40 metres (about 21 feet) in length and weigh over 3.8 tonnes (about 3.75 tons). In this species, the cows rarely grow more than three metres (about ten feet) in length, less than half the size of the bulls. At the beginning of this century, there were scarcely any elephant seals left, as they had been hunted to the brink of extinction. Today, thanks to protection, they again number many thousands and are in no current danger.

Why are they called elephant seals?

The adult males have a kind of trunk or 'proboscis' adorning the nose. When the animal is excited or angry this can be inflated to twice its normal size and begins to look like a miniature version of an elephant's trunk.

The biggest bulls, sometimes called 'beachmasters', fight furiously when defending their harems of females on the breeding beaches. The trunk is then fully inflated and used as part of the elephant seal's threat display.

Are any species of seal or sea lion dangerous?

Not really. Most of them are timid, inquisitive creatures, although tame or injured animals are capable of inflicting a nasty bite if they wish. Even the huge elephant seal is normally a gentle creature, and it is so big and slow-moving on land that it would be quite easy to avoid even if it was angry. One species, the leopard seal, which is found in the waters of the Antarctic, is quite ferocious, at least to other smaller seals and to penguins, both of which it hunts to eat.

Walruses

Are walruses more closely related to seals than to sea lions?

Walruses fall half-way between the families of sea lions and seals. Like the seals they have no external ears, but their shape and the structure of their hind flippers resembles that of sea lions.

Why do they have tusks?

Unlike seals and sea lions, walruses do not feed on fish, but on clams and other shellfish which are found on the seabed. The walrus uses its long ivory tusks to get at this food. Tusks are also used when fighting, especially by the adult male at breeding time.

Do they use their tusks to attack man?

Like so many other animals, the walrus (sometimes known as 'the old man of the sea') is basically a peaceful creature that only wishes to be left alone. But its ivory tusks used to be highly prized by man, and there were many hunting expeditions in the past to the Arctic home of the walrus. When hunted, they will not hesitate to use their formidable tusks to attack and ward off a hunter. Fortunately, nowadays these huge beasts are usually left in peace, and they are slowly recovering their numbers.

What are manatees and dugongs?

These are closely related animals in their own order, the *Sirenia*. Manatees and dugongs are bulky, seal-sized creatures which live in shallow water where they feed entirely on vegetation. They are gentle grazers — which is why they are known as 'sea cows'! They are found either along the sea coast, or in rivers and estuaries, depending on the species. Their most characteristic features are their front limbs, which are broad paddles. In the manatees, the hind end of the animal forms a single broad paddle, while the dugong has a double or fluked tail. Their upper lips are well developed and mobile.

Manatees and dugongs are thought to be the source of legends about mermaids and sirens — mythical creatures of the sea which were said to be half fish and half human, and very beautiful. Although neither dugong nor manatee can be said to be beautiful, they do have a vague human quality, particularly when the female cuddles her single young with the aid of a fore-flipper.

Where do they live?

Manatees are found living in the warm seas and river estuaries of the West Indies and tropical South America, and off the coast of west Africa. Dugongs are found off the east coast of Africa and in shallow water in several areas off the coast of south-east Asia and Australasia. Neither ever come on land as they have no means of moving once they are out of the water.

Are manatees and dugongs rare?

They used to be plentiful along the coasts and river estuaries of a number of tropical countries. They are completely harmless, but many have been killed because people thought they were good to eat. Now they are much less common, and they are extinct in large areas of their former habitat. Today efforts are being made to ensure their protection.

Elephants, rhinoceroses, hippopotami and tapirs

This chapter deals with, among other things, the largest of all land mammals, the elephant. Most of you will probably know that the word 'Jumbo' was in fact the name of a very famous elephant brought to England in Victorian times and admired by thousands at London Zoo. Now we have everything from Jumbo ice-creams to Jumbo jets in memory of the sheer size of this huge animal.

2

This group includes the 'heavyweights' of the land mammals. Elephants are the largest land mammals of all. There are two species, the African and the Indian, although they are not closely related. Five species of rhinoceros exist, two in Africa and three in Asia. The three Asian species of rhino are all very rare. Africa is also the home of the hippopotamus. There are two species, the large Nile hippopotamus which lives in many of the rivers and swamps of Africa, and the smaller and less well known pigmy hippopotamus of west Africa. Tapirs are about the same size as large pigs. Three species are found in South and Central America and one in Malaya. Like hippos, they spend part of their time in marshy areas and in water; they are good swimmers, but they also move about freely on land.

All the animals included in this chapter are vegetarian, feeding on grass and a variety of other plants, leaves and shoots. Tapirs and four of the five rhino species are browsers, feeding on the leaves and branches of trees and bushes within their reach. The hippos and the white rhinoceros are grazing animals. Elephants use both methods of feeding; their long mobile trunks can obtain food at ground level and also at various heights above the ground.

How can you distinguish the African elephant from the Indian elephant?

The African elephant is larger overall than the Indian

African elephant

Indian elephant

species. If you look at it from the side, you can see that it has a hollow or dipped back. It also has much larger and more rounded ears and a less domed head. On each hind foot the African elephant has only three toes, in contrast to four in the Indian species. On the end of its trunk the African elephant has two finger-like projections, whereas the Indian has only one. The African elephant is generally recognized to have two subspecies; the larger bush elephant and the rather smaller forest elephant. But the differences between them are very minor compared with the differences between the elephants of the two continents.

Is it true than only the Indian elephant can be domesticated?

No. Although Indian elephants are better known for their services to man, the African elephant has also been domesticated quite successfully in the past. For example, it is widely accepted by historians that the elephants which crossed the Alps with the Roman general Hannibal's army were African, not Indian. They were probably obtained from north Africa, where elephants are no longer found. Even today, African elephants are used as work animals in some parts of Africa.

Are elephants really scared of mice?

Tests have been made on captive elephants to try to prove or disprove this popular tale. In fact, it seems that elephants are quite unafraid not only of mice but also of snakes and other small creatures. But they do have poor eyesight, and often react with alarm to anything strange which their hearing or sense of smell suggests may be a danger. So a small unexpected sound or movement may cause an elephant to panic for what appears to be no reason.

Do elephants have any enemies?

Full-grown elephants are so large and strong that no other animal will attack or molest them under normal conditions. They truly deserve the title 'king of the beasts'! Young calves are usually well guarded by their mothers and other members of the elephant herd. But a sick or unguarded calf may well fall prey to a lion or a tiger (depending on the country) if it is only a few months old. In the past, of course, man hunted the African elephant for its ivory tusks; even today poaching still continues at an alarming rate in the national parks and reserves, where most elephants now live.

In some parks in east Africa there are large numbers of elephants. They often damage the vegetation and raid surrounding farmlands. When this happens to any great extent the numbers have to be reduced by shooting, because otherwise there is simply not enough food to go round.

Why are elephants destructive?

In the past, elephants were used to living in wide open spaces with the freedom to move where they wished, unrestricted by the boundaries of national parks and reserves. Under such conditions, they were able to feed in one area and then move on. It is when too many elephants become confined in a relatively small area, even if this is a large game park, that the trouble starts. Elephants are wasteful feeders. They knock down trees in order to get at the fruit and leaves, or rip off the bark, killing the trees in the process. When elephants are restricted to one area, the vegetation never has a chance to recover. Not only the elephants but all the other browsing creatures suffer, since they too are losing their food source. The number of elephants has to be reduced or more space given to them, if the balance of animals to vegetation is not to be completely upset.

Do all elephants grow tusks?

In the African elephant both the males and the females grow tusk. But the tusks of the adult males (bulls) are both longer and heavier, so ivory hunters have traditionally pursued the bulls. This has greatly reduced the quality of African elephant tusks: the bulls with the largest tusks were invariably killed, so they could not pass on their fine characteristics to future generations.

In the Indian elephant only the bulls have tusks, and a proportion of Indian bulls grow no tusks at all, or only one. Female Indian elephants possess 'tushes' — small tooth-like projections, which are rarely more than a few centimetres long and are not curved like the tusks of the bulls.

The tusks of an elephant start to grow soon after birth, although they may not break through the skin for some time. They normally continue to grow throughout the elephant's life.

It is true that each elephant has a favourite tusk?

It does seem to be the case that elephants are 'left-handed' or 'right-handed' with their tusks — rather like us. The tusks are used for a variety of purposes — for digging the ground, for removing bark from trees, for using as a 'trunk rest' and for carrying things. Frequently the wear on an elephant's tusks appears unequal. This may be due simply to uneven growth, since a pair of tusks do not always grow to the same shape or length. But often one tusk becomes smooth and polished and may be shorter or blunter than the other, which suggests that the elephant uses it more.

How long do elephants live?

Roughly the same length of time as man. The life of an elephant is governed by its teeth, particularly by the large grinding teeth on which it depends for chewing up tough and fibrous vegetation. As one set of these teeth becomes worn down by chewing, another set grows to take its place. But the elephant can have only six sets of these teeth. When the last set becomes worn, the elephant will eventually die from weakness caused by a combination of hunger and advanced old age. This happens at the age of 60 to 70 years.

Do elephants really go to die in 'elephant graveyards'?

This story has no real foundation, but many people have searched for such places because of the fortune in ivory that would be waiting for them if such a place were found. Most elephants do move away from their herd as old age advances in order to die quietly on their own in the forest. Many die in swamps and river beds, since they come to such places to live out their last months feeding on the lush, soft vegetation which is all that their worn teeth can cope with. As they become weaker the elephants often become bogged down in swampy land by their great weight, and finally die there. Their remains get washed away or sink into the mud, and are hardly ever found. What is rather curious is that a herd of elephants coming across the bones of a dead elephant will often carry the bones away and scatter them, as if trying to bury the remains. Such interest in the dead is unusual in the animal kingdom.

Who are the leaders in elephant society?

Recent studies of the African elephant have shown that the herds are led by adult females known as 'matriarchs'. Each matriarch is usually the eldest female in her group, many of which are related to her directly. The matriarch is the undisputed leader, but she may be assisted by another adult female who acts as a sort of second-in-command. Several of these female groups may join together temporarily to form a larger herd. Young males are cast out of their family groups at the age of 10 or 12 years. They form looser groupings, with other young males, which have no real leader. The oldest bulls often live a solitary existence, or associate with one or more male companions. They join the female groups only to mate. But even then they are not really members of the group, and they never take the role of 'leader of the herd'.

Is it true that elephants never forget?

Elephants are certainly highly intelligent creatures, and they do seem to have good memories. When trained for work they are capable of obeying and remembering quite a wide range of complex orders and activities, and there is evidence that in the wild, they have a well developed social organization. Elephants can recognize other elephants even when they meet only once every few months, and they are capable of providing effective aid to any stricken member of their group. In captivity, elephants have recognized people or surroundings after many years' absence. It is also believed that they hold grudges, for example against another elephant or against a keeper who has wronged them; they will choose their moment to pay back an old score, sometimes after several years have elapsed. However, we cannot say for certain that they think or feel about such things in the same way as we do!

What are the elephant's nearest relatives?

The elephant is a bit of an odd-man-out. Even the two existing species are not very closely related. The African elephant's closest relative after the Indian elephant is a surprisingly small animal called a hyrax, which also lives in Africa. Hyraxes are rodent-like animals about the size of a hare.

Which is the largest of the rhinoceroses?

The white rhinoceros, one of the two African species. It may stand up to 1.52 metres (about six feet) high at the shoulder, and after the elephant it is the second largest land mammal.

Which is the rarest species of rhinoceros?

All three of the species which are found in Asia are rare and in danger of extinction. However there are several hundred great Indian rhinoceroses. This is a species found in several reserves in Nepal and Assam, where it lives principally in thick marshes. Under protection, it has increased in number over the last few years, but it is still not entirely safe from poaching. The Sumatran rhinoceros is found in the jungles of Indonesia. Because it is a shy forest dweller, it is very hard to count its numbers or provide it with effective protection. It is believed there may be 100 or more of these rhinos. Rarest of the three species is the Javan rhino, which is only known to exist for sure in the Udjong Kulong reserve in western Java. In the Udjong Kulong reserve, the Javan rhinos are strictly protected and their numbers are slowly increasing. But the most recent estimates indicate only 50 or 60 animals.

What are the differences between the African black and white rhinos?

In spite of their names, the differences are not in the colours. Both species are in fact grey. 'White' comes from the Afrikaans word 'wied', meaning 'wide', and refers to the white rhino's mouth. The white rhino is a grazing species, and it has a high shoulder hump and a square or 'wide' lip to allow it to use its massive head for grazing grass. The black rhino is altogether more lightly built. It browses on leaves and vegetation at shoulder height, and has a hook-shaped upper lip for this purpose. White rhinos normally live in groups or herds. In contrast, the black rhino is usually encountered alone, or is found in small groups, perhaps a mother and calf together with an older youngster, or a pair of adults temporarily living together. The black rhino is a much more aggressive and temperamental animal than the more placid white rhino.

White rhinoceros

Is it true that rhinos are nearly blind?

Rhinos do depend more on their senses of hearing and smell than on their eyesight, but at short range they can see quite well. A rhino often charges because it is unsure what has disturbed it — rather like the elephant with the mouse. Frequently it merely comes forward to investigate and then departs when satisfied that there is no danger. But an angry rhino will charge, lowering its head and striking upwards with its horn at the last minute. It is often thought that one has only to sidestep a charging rhino and it will blunder past, but if a rhino really means business it can turn very quickly.

What are the horns of the rhinoceros made of?

The horns are not true horns at all. They are made of compressed *hair*! They grow in much the same way as our hair or nails, but in the shape and texture come to resemble the horns of other animals such as goats. The smooth pointed shape comes from the rhino rubbing its horns on anthills and on the ground. The horns continue to grow throughout the animal's life. Horns over 1.27 metres (about fifty inches) long have been recorded in black rhinos. Normally the front horn is the longer of the two horns.

Do all rhinos have two horns?

The two African species and the Sumatran rhinoceros of Asia all have two horns, but in the Sumatran rhino the second horn may be almost nonexistent. Hence there is sometimes confusion between the Sumatran and the one-horned Javan rhino. The Indian rhino is a larger version of the Javan species, which it resembles closely, and it too has only a single horn which is rarely more than a few centimetres long.

Can a rhinoceros toss a man in the air?

The only species likely to do this is the black rhino, which is rather bad tempered and will charge and attack people or even cars if molested. It is quite capable of killing a man with its horns. The Asian rhinos attack in a different way, using the sharp 'tushes' in their lower jaws and slashing upwards to create a nasty wound. All rhinos are normally quite peaceful and timid if unmolested.

Why are rhinoceroses killed for their horns?

In some parts of the world rhinoceros horn is thought to possess magical properties. For this reason all species have been hunted, and have faced extinction. The horn is usually ground into powder and then smuggled into countries where high prices are paid for it. Illegal poaching of all species still goes on.

What are the chief enemies of the rhinos, apart from man?

In the wild, grown rhinos have few natural enemies. They are so large and thick-skinned that few animals would dare attack a healthyadult. But the very young calves do feature on the menu of some of the fiercer members of the animal kingdom. In Africa, lions and hyaenas will try to take a very young or sickly rhino calf away from its mother. In Asia, it is the tigers. The bodies of rhinos that have died naturally, or have been shot by hunters, may be picked over by a number of scavenging animals, such as vultures and jackals, provided that a larger animal such as a lion or hyaena can first break open the very tough skin.

Why do tick birds often accompany rhinos and perch on them?

Tick birds, or oxpeckers, provide a double service to the rhino. Firstly, they feed on the various insects living in the rhino's skin. Secondly they provide the short-sighted rhino with an early warning system, since their alarm calls give him a warning of possible danger.

How many species of hippopotamus are there?

Two, both of which live in Africa. The large Nile hippopotamus lives near rivers and lakes over a large part of Africa, and is the species most commonly seen in zoos, books and films. The pigmy hippopotamus lives near rivers and streams in forested parts of west Africa, and is much more rare.

What are the chief differences between the two species?

The Nile hippopotamus is much the larger of the two — about the size of a small rhino. It spends most of the day in water, coming ashore at night to feed on grass and other vegetation. The pigmy hippo is not much bigger than a large pig. It is less ungainly in appearance with a smaller head and longer legs for the size of its body. It has a smooth, shiny skin, which is almost black. It spends a lot more time on land than the Nile hippo does, but it is rarely seen because it lives along the sides of rivers and streams in forested areas.

Are hippos rare?

The Nile hippo can be found in great numbers in some parts of Africa, and certain rivers and lakes contain

Nile hippopotamus

large herds of them. In some of these places the hippos create havoc, since at night they leave the water and move out into the surrounding bush to eat. Each hippo requires over a hundred kilogrammes of vegetation per night, so you can imagine what a whole herd will eat! In national parks and reserves, large numbers of feeding hippos can reduce the area for miles around a river or lake to almost desert conditions, since they graze extensively at ground level. Elsewhere they do great damage to crops and farmlands. In each case, the only effective solution is to reduce their numbers by shooting.

Pigmy hippos are found only in a relatively small area of west Africa. They live on their own or in pairs, never in large herds. No one has ever managed to count them properly, but there is concern that the cutting down of forests for timber could prove a danger to their survival.

Are hippos aggressive?

The large Nile hippo is an unpredictable and rather quarrelsome creature. The large bulls fight among themselves, often inflicting terrible wounds on each other with their great tusks. Normally they are calm in the presence of man, but in areas where they have been regularly harassed or hunted, they learn to fear man and may attack if provoked. The bulls are quite capable of attacking and overturning a small boat, and then attacking the occupants. They are also very cunning, sinking quietly under the water and then surfacing near a boat and ramming it at full speed using their enormous weight and powerful tusks.

What is a 'water horse'?

This is an alternative name for the Nile hippopotamus. Hippos are not closely related to horses, but they do resemble them in a rather grotesque way. Although they appear clumsy on land, under the water their movements are graceful, as they glide through the water or walk along the bottom. Their nostrils and eyes are on the top of their heads, which allows them to remain submerged almost totally even when they rise to the surface to breathe.

Tapirs look rather like a cross between a pig and an elephant. Which of these are they most closely related to?

Tapirs have a family of their own, the *Tapiridae*. Despite their appearance, they are not closely related to either pigs or elephants. Their evolution shows that they are among the oldest species of mammal on earth. The short mobile trunk is used in the same way as the elephant's, but its short length restricts the number of uses to which it can be put.

What colour are tapirs?

The adults of the South and central American species are a uniform blackish-brown colour, with white tips to the ears in some cases. The mountain tapir has a more woolly coat than the short-haired Brazilian species. The Malayan tapir is coloured black and white in a distinctive and sharply contrasting pattern. Young tapirs are heavily spotted and striped with white at birth. As the tapir grows up, the pattern of white markings fades away, leaving the more uniform colour or colours of the adult.

Why is it that only the young tapirs have these spots and stripes?

We think that the spots and stripes provide an effective pattern of camouflage, which is lost as the animal grows older and can rely on other means of avoiding danger. It is interesting to note that while the adult South American tapirs are different in colour from the

Malayan tapir

Malayan tapirs, the young of all the species share this distinct striped and spotted pattern.

What is camouflage?

Camouflage is the word for the ability of an animal to blend in with its surroundings, usually because its colouring or marking closely resembles its background. A great variety of mammals, birds, reptiles and insects use this method to help them survive, either when avoiding predators or when trying to remain hidden when hunting other animals.

Are tapirs rare?

The Malayan and Brazilian tapirs still exist in reasonable numbers. But they are hunted for their flesh and there is concern that their numbers may now be decreasing rapidly. The other South American species are much rarer. Perhaps they have never been common, for relatively little is known about them.

What do tapirs eat?

Tapirs are entirely vegetarian, feeding on a wide range of fruits and herbs and on the leaves of trees and bushes. They also feed on succulent plants which grow in the water. Tapirs are shy, secretive animals, and they spend most of the daylight hours resting in thick cover, emerging to swim and feed at dusk.

Are tapirs dangerous?

Tapirs have sharp teeth which they may use if cornered by other animals. A number of American tapirs have been found with scars to prove that they are even able to beat off an attack by their chief enemy, the jaguar. Tapirs rarely attack man, preferring to run away whenever possible, but their sharp teeth and the toenails of the front feet can be used to advantage if the animal is hard pressed.

What are the chief enemies of tapirs?

In South and central America, tapirs are preyed on mainly by the jaguar, and form one of its main foods. Although tapirs can run quite fast and swim very well (even submerging, rather like the hippo) a determined jaguar is quite capable of killing one. The Malayan tapir is preyed on by tigers, and also by leopards, where these big cats still survive.

Horses, asses and zebras

Horses and asses have for a long time been excellent workmates with man. They are tremendously strong and willing animals, if a little stubborn at first during training. There have been almost as many famous horses as famous entertainers. Think of Champion, Black Beauty or Red Rum. There are also lots of tales and folklores which have arisen around horses, donkeys and asses. For example, there is a breed of ass in Ireland which has a prominent cross on its back. The story goes that they are all related to the ass that carried Jesus of Nazareth into Jerusalem.

3

The horses and their close relatives, the asses and zebras, are among the most fleet-footed of all the hoofed mammals. They are long-legged, powerful creatures built for speed and endurance, which are their chief methods of avoiding danger. Their hooves are actually elongated middle toes, surrounded by horny casing. Although the earliest forms of horses possessed five toes, these have been reduced to two small splints, one each side of the enlarged middle toe on each foot.

All members of this family are grazing animals. Consequently they are found in open plains and grasslands, and some in semi-desert conditions. Wild horses, from which our domestic animals (whatever their shape or size) are descended, are now only found in Asia. Several species of wild asses exist, in Asia and in Africa, and one of these is thought to be the ancestor of our domestic donkey. Zebras are confined to grasslands and the semi-desert in Africa, where several different species can be found.

All these animals normally live in groups or larger herds, but the social organization is not the same in all species. The females in each case produce single young, normally at intervals of a year; like the young of other hoofed animals, these are able to stand and run soon after birth, a necessary means of evading predators.

Przewalski's horse

How many species of wild horse are found living today?

Only one. This is the Mongolian wild horse, often known as Przewalski's horse after the Russian explorer who first described it. Przewalski's horses exist only in the Altai-Gobi region of Mongolia, a vast windswept region of barren mountains and plains, where the horses exist under very bleak conditions.

Are these horses rare?

In the wild they are very rare indeed and are even thought to be extinct. Possibly many more exist in captivity than in the wild, for they are easy to keep and breed and there are now several hundred in the zoos of the world. But here there is a danger that close inbreeding may result in a type of horse which is inferior to (or at least different in appearance from) its wild counterpart. This is because all the wild horses in captivity are closely related, being descended from a small number of original animals.

Why are the wild horses so rare?

In spite of living in such a remote area these horses have suffered from hunting by local tribesmen in the past. Even now, despite rigorous protection, it is not easy to enforce hunting laws in such out of the way places. The last herds have also been driven away from the watering places so vital to them: settlements are encroaching upon the horses' last home. Because the wild horse is closely related to the domestic animal, it will interbreed with it. Where there are herds of domestic horses living near to wild horses, wild stallions sometimes 'steal' these herds. They fight the domestic stallions off and then take over the females. The result is a number of cross-bred horses intermingled with the true wild ones. This further affects the survival of the wild horse as a true species.

Is the Mongolian wild horse the ancestor of the domestic horse?

Yes, amongst others. Certainly many of the tough little horses of Asia still bear a close resemblance to this species, and even the British Exmoor pony bears a number of likenesses.

Another species of wild horse, the tarpan, is also an ancestor of the domestic horse. It once inhabited the forests and grasslands of Europe, but it is now extinct. It was similar in appearance to the Mongolian wild horse, but grey rather than brown.

How does the Mongolian wild horse differ from our domestic varieties?

The Mongolian wild horse is a stocky animal, the size of a pony. It is light brown all over, with horizontal dark stripes on the legs. It also has a dark stripe running along the spine, and a pale or 'mealy' muzzle. Unlike domestic horses, it has a stiff upright mane like a zebra. In the summer it has a short, smooth coat which is replaced for the cold winter by a longer shaggier growth of hair. in its habits and temperament, however, the wild horse closely resembles the domestic horse. It has even been broken to the saddle, although this is exceptional. Domestic horses on the other hand vary tremendously in size, shape and colour, because of selective breeding by man. Although the Exmoor pony is really quite similar to its wild ancestor.

Are there wild horses in other parts of the world?

The mustangs of North America, the brumbies of Australia and many other breeds of 'wild' horse are not genuine wild animals. They are 'feral' horses — that is horses decended from animals kept by man which have escaped or have been allowed to run wild. Their descendants may now live a completely wild existence, and be difficult to tame, but they are nevertheless domestic not wild horses.

The ponies which live in various parts of Britain are also not truly wild, although often termed 'wild ponies'. Despite living on their own much of the year they are rounded up from time to time to be branded or sold. They are often trained as riding ponies. Also they are often fed additional rations during hard weather and cannot be regarded as living a truly wild existence.

How do true wild horses live in their natural surroundings?

Wild horses live in small bands, each of which comprises a stallion, his mares and foals and a few yearlings (year-old horses). The stallion acts as a scout and protector for his group and will lead the group away from danger or defend it from hunters (human or animal) or the advances of rival stallions. Young males are ousted from the group by the adult stallion as they approach maturity. They often form bachelor groups each comprising several males. When old enough, they will fight for possession of another stallion's herd, or perhaps start with a single mare as the basis for their own herd.

It is interesting to note that domestic horses, when allowed to live under natural conditions without close supervision, also have the same social groupings. The so called 'wild' ponies of Britain often live like this almost the whole year round.

What do true wild horses find to eat in their inhospitable homeland?

Although wild horses, and asses too, live in areas where the vegetation is poor and tough, they are equipped to feed and thrive on such meagre fare. But they do need water to survive, amd they move to drinking places every two or three days at the least. In the past they have been hunted at their watering places, and they now face the problem that many of their traditional watering places have been taken over by man.

How many species of wild ass are there?

Scientists frequently disagree over exactly how many separate species of ass there are. Three species live in Asia — the kiang of Tibet, the Indian wild ass, and the Persian onager. All these are rather similar, but a fourth species, the kulan, is so similar to the onager that it may not be a separate species, but merely a race of the onager. In Africa there are, or were, two species, here again similar to each other. These are the Somalia wild ass, found in Somalia and Ethiopia, and the Nubian wild ass which is now almost certainly extinct. All the other wild asses only exist in small numbers.

Indian wild ass

Why are wild asses so rare?

For the same reasons that apply to the wild horses: hunting, man's general interference with their habitat, and the loss of safe watering places. In Africa they have interbred with domestic donkeys, which resulted in a number of 'impure' animals.

How do wild asses differ from domestic donkeys?

While the wild asses are basically similar in appearance to domestic donkeys, they are really quite unlike the gentle, hardworking donkey we know so well. They are taller and more finely built and have terrific speed and great stamina. The domestic donkey has inherited the stamina, but centuries of domestication have reduced its speed. The Asian asses are a sandy brown colour, with a dark back-stripe and a short, stiff mane. The Somali wild ass is a beautiful pinkish-grey colour with dark, zebra-like markings on its legs. The Nubian species was similar in appearance, but in addition had a thin black stripe across the shoulders. For this reason, it is commonly thought that this was the ancestor of domestic donkeys, many of which have the well known 'cross' on their shoulders.

Are donkeys and asses really stubborn?

Asses and donkeys appear to be rather less intelligent than horses, and consequently less easy to train. Domestic donkeys are patient, gentle creatures that seem to have lost the spirit of their wild relatives. But they have great stamina and only become stubborn or embittered if ill-treated. In the past they were often crossed with horses to produce mules, which were considered to combine the intelligence of the horse with the stamina of the donkey. Wild asses are not easily tamed, being rather nervous creatures. However, the stallions will fight aggressively amongst themselves for possession of the females.

What are the main enemies of wild horses and asses?

Undoubtedly man is the greatest enemy. There are very few large predators in the areas where these animals live, and hardly any of them would be able to catch up with them in any case! Wild horses and asses can keep up a fast gallop for long periods of time when they need to. Only man with his motor vehicles and rifles can have any real effect on their populations — and he has already done so.

Since horses and asses usually live in open areas, and have keen senses of sight and hearing, they can usually spot any danger a long distance off and then gallop right way from it. Wild horses and Asiatic asses may occasionally be preyed upon by wolves, but only a small foal or an old or sickly adult is likely to be caught. Even then, the stallion of a herd will often defend his group very effectively with a combination of hooves and teeth.

How many species of zebra are there?

Zebras are divided into three main types. The mountain zebras of South Africa, the plains (or common) zebras of east Africa, and the large Grevy's zebras of northern Kenya and Ethiopia.

How can you tell them apart?

The plains zebras of east Africa can be found in large herds on the plains and in many game parks and reserves. This is the species seen most frequently in captivity. It is the most horse-like of all the zebras, since is has a head like a horse with small ears, and stands as tall as a small pony. Actually there are several different types or races of the common (or plains) zebra, but the differences are only in the patterning of their stripes. In all the common zebras the stripes are broad bands of black which meet under the belly and are wide on the rump.

The Grevy's and mountain zebras are more ass-like in appearance, with long ears, a head like an ass and taller proportions. The Grevy's zebra has a beautiful pattern of very thin stripes and is larger than the other species. The mountain zebras of South Africa are midway in appearance between the Grevy's and common zebras. The stripes are broad on the rump but relatively narrow on the rest of the body. Most distinctive is the 'gridiron' pattern of stripes above the base of the tail, which is found only in the mountain zebras, as is the flap or 'dewlap' of skin under the throat. Curiously, no two zebras, even of the same species, are striped in exactly the same pattern!

Which is the rarest of the zebras?

The Cape mountain zebra, one of the two mountain zebra species living in South Africa, is very rare. Thirty years ago it was in grave danger of extinction and numbered only a few dozen animals. Today, thanks to reserves created specially for its protection, its numbers are slowly increasing. The slightly larger Hartmann's mountain zebra of south-west Africa still numbers several thousand animals. But many of them exist outside reserves, for example in the inhospitable Namib desert. Consequently, it too is considered to be in some danger.

The Grevy's zebra could be found in good numbers until recently, in parts of northern Kenya and Ethiopia. But now is seems to be approaching extinction for reasons not yet fully understood. Measures are now being taken to try to ensure increased protection for this species.

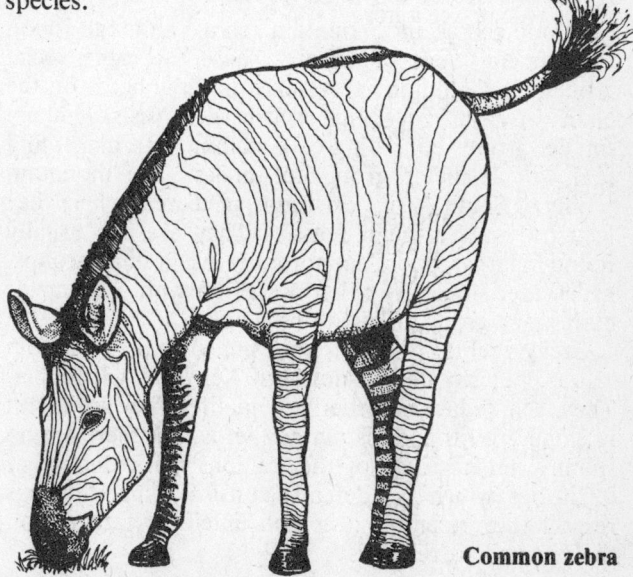

Common zebra

Why do zebras have stripes?

It does seem odd for an animal with several natural enemies to have such bold markings. Some people believe that the bold pattern of stripes confuses the enemy. Another theory is that the stripes act as camouflage. During the day, in the heat-haze and dust of the African plains, zebras at a distance often look grey, as the colours blend together and the zebras become an indistinct blur in their surroundings. These 'grey' animals might be overlooked by a hunting lion, or pack of wild dogs. At night, the black and white pattern may blend with the moonlight and shadows on the plains, again making the zebras less obvious. It is also thought that the striping patterns may help zebras to identify each other.

Do all zebras live in the same way?

Common zebras and mountain zebras, although found in different types of terrain, share the same social groupings. Common zebras exist in large herds on the plains of east Africa, but each herd consists of many smaller groups consisting of a stallion with mares and foals, or bachelor groups of males. The mountain zebras of South Africa exist in rugged areas where they feed on sparse, tough grasses. They are not usually found in larger herds, but normally live in small groups, which are, similarly, either a stallion with a group of mares, or a group of bachelor males.

Grevy's zebras exist in terrain similar to the mountain zebras, but situated in northern Kenya and Ethiopia. They seem to lack an orderly social life. They are found in small groups and also larger herds, but there are no 'family' units. Some of the stallions mark out larger territories, which they defend against rival males. In this respect they resemble deer and antelope, rather than their immediate relatives.

What are the main enemies of zebras?

Common zebras are hunted by lions, hunting dogs and hyaenas. Leopards and cheetahs will hunt and kill foals on occasion. In some parts of east Africa, zebras form the major part of the lion's diet. Certainly they are one of the most preyed upon animals on the African plains, where they exist in large numbers.

Mountain and Grevy's zebras exist in areas where there are relatively fewer predators capable of killing them, although they are occasionally taken by lions or hunting dogs where these species also occur. In the case of the mountain zebras, especially the Cape species, their rarity is very much the result of man's influence in the past. We don't quite know why Grevy's zebras are so rare, but poaching is undoubtedly one of the reasons.

Are any zebras already extinct?

Yes. The quagga became extinct during the last century. It was the same size and build as the common zebra, and we are not sure whether it was a race of this species or an entirely different species. It was unlike other zebras in that it was brown, not white, and the dark stripes were restricted to the head, neck, and foreparts of the body.

Burchell's zebra, the southernmost race of the common zebra, became extinct at the beginning of this century.

Why did the quagga become extinct?

The quagga formerly existed in large numbers in South Africa, but was hunted out of existence by 1880. After that a few still existed in zoos, but no real effort was made to breed from them, since nobody realized that they were almost extinct in the wild. One by one, these last captive quaggas died. Now all we have by which to remember the quagga are a few faded photographs and under 20 museum specimens around the world. There is one in the Natural History Museum at Tring, Hertfordshire.

How do zebras defend themselves?

They rely on good sight and hearing to detect danger,

and speed to avoid it. If cornered or defending their young, they will fight with teeth and hooves. When attacked by lions or wild dogs they sometimes put up a valiant fight, and they may even succeed in warding off an attack by a solitary lion or a very small pack of wild dogs.

What sound do zebras make?

Common zebras have a barking call. The mountain zebra has a high-pitched scream or whinny, which is rather like the neigh of a frightened horse. Grevy's zebra has a loud donkey-like bray, starting with a series of grunts.

Can zebras be domesticated?

Zebras have been tamed and trained on a number of occasions, but it takes a great deal of patience and skill for they are nervous, temperamental creatures. Zebras have also been broken to the saddle. They are sometimes seen performing in circuses, but they rarely do more than trot around the ring and look decorative, for they are difficult to school in the manner of performing horses.

Can zebras be crossed with horses or donkeys?

Zebras can be crossed with both horses and donkeys, but the offspring are infertile (nature's way of ensuring that this biological 'mistake' is not continued in future generations!). Known as 'zebroids' or 'zedonks' these offspring vary in appearance according to their parentage. Usually they are plain coloured, with stripes on head, neck and legs, and perhaps faint stripes on the body.

In the past, the large Grevy's zebra was deliberately crossed with horses, in an attempt to combine the stamina and resistance to disease of the zebra with the docile nature of the horse. These animals were used for drawing vehicles, but with varying success. Grevy's zebra is the only species big and strong enough to make such a cross worthwhile.

Will zebras of different species interbreed?

This never seems to happen in the wild. In most cases, the different species have different habitats and never meet. In parts of Kenya, Grevy's zebra and the smaller common zebra sometimes occur in mixed herds, but within these herds each species keeps to its own kind, and crosses between them have never been recorded.

In captivity, the mountain zebra has been crossed with the common zebra. Grevy's zebra seems unwilling to cross with other species of zebra, although it is not difficult to cross it with a horse. The several different races of common zebra, on the other hand, interbreed freely in captivity.

Antelope, deer, cattle, giraffes and okapi

*Those with a taste for tall stories may like to hear about George. In this case the story is both tall and true. George was a male (or rather bull) giraffe imported to Chester Zoo from Kenya in the late 1950's. At the tender age of nine he narrowly missed bumping his head on the ceiling of the giraffe house which was 6.09 metres (20 feet) high. If you can't imagine that, then think of George easily licking the **top** of a double-decker bus, with lots of room to spare! That placed George as the tallest giraffe ever recorded, although there probably have been taller giraffes, but they were a little difficult to measure I should imagine.*

Rolf Harris

4

This group of animals is composed of 'even-toed ungulates' — that is, they have split or cloven hooves (unlike the horse family, whose hooves are single and undivided). They fall into several different families, but all of them are ruminants — that is animals which 'chew the cud' as part of their digestive process.

A large number of different species of antelope and deer exist, and several varieties of wild cattle. There are so many species of deer and antelope that it is not possible to describe them all here. The giraffe and its only relation, the okapi, have their own family, the *Giraffidae*.

The young of these animals are born singly, with very few exceptions. They can run or walk soon after birth, although many depend on concealment for their survival during the early weeks of life.

All are vegetarians. Some, including many of the deer and some of the cattle and antelope, are grazing animals. The giraffe, okapi and several species of antelope are browsing animals. Antelope are found principally in Africa and Asia, with one species in North America. Deer are found in Asia and the Americas, and wild cattle in Asia, Africa and North America.

What are the chief differences between antelope and deer?

Antelope grow one set of horns, which go on growing throughout their lifetime and are never shed. These horns consist of a bony growth from the skull surrounded by a casing of true horn. Deer's horns are called antlers. These are grown and shed each year, are often branched and consist entirely of bone. The females of many species of antelope bear horns, while only the reindeer of Scandinavia, and its close relative the caribou (of North America), bear antlers in both sexes. On rare occasions females of the roe deer species also grow antlers.

What are the correct terms for male, female and young antelope?

The members of the larger species of antelope, such as eland, wildebeest, oryx and kudu, are called bulls, cows and calves respectively. Members of the middle-sized antelope species are usually described as bucks, does and fawns.

Common eland

Which is the largest species of antelope?

The giant, or Lord Derby's eland stands as tall as a cow. This magnificent animal is confined to a few forested regions of Africa and is believed to be rare. Its much more common relation, the common eland, is almost as big and is frequently seen in captivity.

Do antelope live in grasslands or in forests?

Antelope are a very versatile group of animals. The large number of different species are found in a wide range of habitats, varying from thick forests, woodlands and marshes, to grassland and desert. In Africa there is an antelope species for virtually every type of habitat.

Which is the smallest antelope?

Two groups of African antelope, known as duikers and dik-diks, contain species which are very small indeed. But the royal antelope of Africa, which is found living in the thick vegetation at the edges of jungles, is the tiniest of all. It stands only 25-30.5 centimetres (10-12 inches) tall!

Which is the rarest of the antelope?

Several species exist only in small numbers and are considered rare. But the Arabian oryx, one of the several species of oryx and the only one found outside Africa, is probably the rarest of all. Although it is a very fast animal, it could not escape from hunters in fast cars and aeroplanes. Fortunately, some were already in captivity and an expedition to capture more animals has been successful. Several captive herds now exist, both in Arabia and in America.

How do antelope avoid predators?

Many of the medium-sized and smaller antelope form the main diet of several predatory animals. The plains-dwelling species rely on their keen senses of sight, hearing and smell to warn them of danger. In many species a few members of the herd act as look-outs, while others are feeding. Plains antelope are very swift runners and this is their chief method of evading capture. Forest antelope rely chiefly on camouflage as they are not such fast runners. They have patterned coats which help them to blend with the vegetation. Their hearing is also very acute — most of them have large, fan-like ears to help them pick up the slightest sound.

Which antelope occurs in the largest numbers?

The brindled gnu or wildebeest occurs in huge concentrations, often mixed with zebra, on the east African plains. Each year, in the dry season, these antelope migrate in great numbers to areas where fresh grazing and water are available.

Which is the fastest of the antelope?

Many of the plains antelope are very fast runners. The North American pronghorn has clocked up speeds of around 100 kilometres per hour when hard pressed. The black buck of India can sometimes outrun a cheetah, which is the only animal capable of catching it. The impala, another medium-sized antelope from Africa, is also very fast. It is even better known for its leaping ability. When frightened or pursued, impala run in a series of huge leaps, sometimes covering a distance of about 12 metres (40 feet) in one bound. They have been known to clear around 4.5 metres (16 feet) from a standing jump.

Can antelope be domesticated?

The common eland of Africa is the only species which has been domesticated successfully. Eland provide very good meat and the females can be milked like cattle.

Because eland are native to Africa, they are resistant to many African diseases and can also thrive on relatively poor grazing. They are now farmed commercially in Africa as a good alternative to real cattle, which are more vulnerable to diseases and need lush grass.

Are there any deer in Africa?

Only one species. The Barbary stag (a race of the red deer) is found in a few areas north of the Sahara. Deer are chiefly creatures of cooler forested regions.

How many species of deer live in Britain?

Two species, the large red deer and the smaller roe deer, are native to Britain. The fallow deer was introduced into Britain so long ago that it too may be considered a native. The sika deer was introduced from Japan much more recently, but it is now well established in several places in Britain. The small muntjac and Chinese water deer both originate from Asia, but both seem quite at home here.

Roe deer

Fallow deer

Do all deer species have antlers?

Two of the small Asian species, the musk deer and the Chinese water deer, bear no antlers at all. Instead the males of both of these species have long canine teeth in their upper jaws. These sharp 'tusks' are used for fighting and as a means of defence.

How are the antlers produced?

The growth of deer antlers represents one of the most amazing feats of nature. It takes only a few months for a deer to grow its antlers. While growing, they are covered in a fine covering of soft skin known as 'velvet'. This protects the growing bone and also supplies the antlers with blood and tissue for their development. When fully developed the antler bone hardens and the velvet is rubbed off. A few months after they are grown, the antlers drop off and the whole process is repeated again in the following year!

Normally the antlers start to grow when the deer is one year old. The first ones are simple spikes and the sets grow larger and more complicated as the animal gets older. After the deer has passed its prime, the antlers get less impressive as the years go by. However, the size and complexity of the antlers is only a rough guide to the deer's age. Rich feeding can often produce enormous antlers with many forks and branches, while poor feeding sometimes results in antlers of less than average size, irrespective of the owner's age.

Red deer

What are the antlers used for?

Found almost exclusively in male deer, it seems that antlers are used mainly as a form of display, perhaps to impress or intimidate rival males. In many species the males with the largest antlers are the top-ranking ones. At mating time in many species the males fight for possession of the females. Then the antlers are used in vigorous battles, which are usually quite harmless, despite their apparent ferocity. A few months later the antlers are shed and a new pair start to grow, indicating that their importance is centred around the breeding season.

Which is the largest species of deer?

The moose of North America and Canada and the closely related elk of Scandinavia, both of which stand nearly 1.8 metres (six feet) at the shoulder, are the largest species of deer.

What are the correct names for the males, females and young of deer?

The larger species, such as the moose, North American wapiti (a large relative of the red deer), reindeer and caribou are known as bulls, cows and calves. Red deer and some of the other slightly smaller species such as the Indian sambar and swamp deer are known as stag, hinds and calves. Deer which are smaller still, such as the roe, are termed bucks, does and fawns, although the young may also be referred to as kids. The correct terms vary from species to species and also from country to country.

Can deer be domesticated?

One species — the reindeer of Scandinavia and Lapland — has been domesticated for centuries. The Lapps herd them rather like cattle and rely on them for food, milk and clothing, as well as for pulling sledges. Experiments are taking place in Scotland to see whether red deer can be 'farmed'. These experiments have so far been successful, so we may soon see the red deer used as a farm animal on a commercial basis for its meat, which is known as venison and regarded as a delicacy.

What kinds of deer are seen in parks and the grounds of stately homes?

In Britain these are normally fallow or red deer. Although they have lived in these surroundings for many generations, even for hundreds of years, these deer are not truly domesticated. Despite their tame appearance and civilized habitat, they still behave very much like their counterparts in the wild. Even where deer will approach people to take food from them (as in Richmond Park, Surrey, for example) they can only be called 'semi-tame'.

Are deer dangerous?

Normally deer are timid creatures and are very wary of man. But in parks and the grounds of larger houses, where they have lost some of their inherent fear of man, the males may grow aggressive at breeding time when their mating and protective responses overcome their natural caution. This particularly applies to animals living in close confinement or hand-raised specimens. Such animals have no fear and at mating time the males can become extremely dangerous. There are many reports of 'tame' male deer attacking people, injuring and even killing them.

How many young do deer produce?

Most of them give birth to only a single young. But in some species, such as the moose, twins are quite common; and the roe deer has been known to produce triplets. Even red deer occasionally have twins, but this is very rare. The little Chinese water deer is a striking exception: it can produce up to six or even eight young at a time. This is unique among the deer and antelope families.

Are any species of deer particularly rare?

The Persian fallow deer, a relative of the European species, is found in very small numbers in Iran. Several other Asiatic species of deer only exist in small numbers. One of these, Père David's deer, is a large species from China with a particularly interesting history. It is believed to have become extinct in the wild centuries ago, but there was at one stage still a large herd in the Imperial Hunting Park outside Peking. The first westerner to see these deer was a French missionary, Father David, after whom the species was named. He managed to send a few of them to zoos in Europe. Some time later, a series of man-made and natural disasters destroyed the original herd, leaving less than 20 deer scattered among European zoos. These were then gathered together in England at Woburn Park, home of the Dukes of Bedford. From this tiny nucleus, the deer gradually started to increase again.

How many species of wild cattle are there?

The term 'wild cattle' covers the numerous members of the family *Bovidae*. These are the American and European bison, the buffaloes of Africa and Asia and several species in Asia which are simply called 'wild cattle'.

Are the American and European bison the same species?

No, although they are closely related. The American bison is a massive animal with huge shoulders and a heavy head, equipped for a life of grazing on the open prairies of North America and Canada. It was reduced to the point of extinction by over-hunting by white settlers. Fortunately it was saved and now exists again in reasonable numbers. The European bison is a forest dweller feeding on the leaves and shoots of trees. It has longer legs and a less pronounced shoulder hump than the American species. Once found in forests all over Europe, it is now confined to forest reserves in eastern Europe, chiefly Poland. Both can be seen in zoos, although the American bison is more common.

African buffalo with white egret

Which are the real buffaloes?

The name 'buffalo' applies only to the large, dark, heavy-horned African buffalo and to a similar species in India and Asia. The African, or Cape buffalo, is a heavy, thickset creature with a sullen and aggressive nature. It is commonly regarded as one of the most cunning and dangerous of the African 'big game' animals. In Asia buffaloes have been domesticated by man and are used for meat and milk and for pulling ploughs and carts. The wild buffalo in Asia is less heavily built and has horns of a different shape. Wild buffaloes are sometimes allowed to mate with domestic ones, because it is thought that they improve the domestic species.

What is a yak?

A yak is a kind of cattle which has been domesticated in the same way as the Asian buffalo. It is found in the Himalayas in Tibet, even very high up in the mountains, where its long shaggy coat protects it from the cold climate. The yak is used as a beast of burden, and for its meat and woolly coat. Closely related to domestic cattle, it will breed with them. Yaks of the wild type are still found, but are probably considerably outnumbered by the domestic variety.

Which is the rarest species of wild cattle?

There are several Asian species, such as the gaur, gayal and anoa, which can only be found in small numbers. The anoa is a species of dwarf buffalo found only in Celebes and the Philippine Islands. The kouprey, another Asiatic species found in Cambodia, is even more rare. These animals are very shy and difficult to observe in their forest home. There is a danger that koupreys may soon become extinct if steps are not taken to protect them.

Are there any wild cattle in Britain?

Until recently several herds of wild cattle lived in Britain. These animals are thought to be descendants of a breed of cattle which once roamed Britain but died out a long time ago. Some of them were enclosed in parks, where their descendants have continued to live to this day. Best known and oldest of these are the Chillingham cattle. Records show that the herd has lived in Chillingham Park, Northumberland for centuries, during which time they have never been moved from the area or crossed with other breeds. Certainly the Chillingham cattle, which are white with reddish-brown markings on legs and face, are very wild and entirely self-supporting. But even this herd is not considered truly wild, because their ancestors are thought to have been a very ancient breed of domestic cattle, rather than a genuinely wild species.

Why does the giraffe have such a long neck?

So that it can reach up for leaves growing high in the trees. Since much of the giraffe's diet consists of tough, prickly foliage (such as leaves of the thorny acacia tree), it is also equipped with rubbery lips and a long tongue

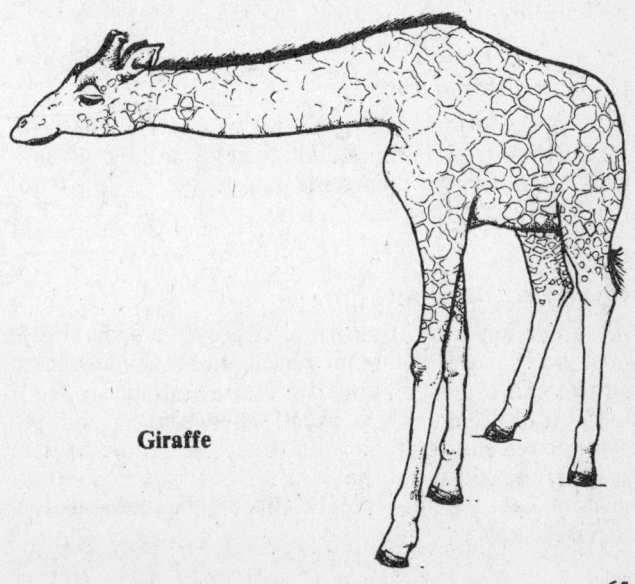

Giraffe

which allow it to pull off the tough spiky leaves and then eat them without hurting its mouth.

Where are giraffes found in the wild?

Only in Africa, where they are found living in small groups on the plains. Since they exist almost entirely on the foliage of tall trees, they usually live in relatively open areas where they can get at the trees, rather than in thick forests.

How many species of giraffe are there?

All giraffes belong to a single species, but several different races exist, which differ chiefly in the colour and pattern of the coat. In some races the coat is blotched with small, distinct spots. In others the markings are larger and more irregular. The reticulated giraffe of northern Kenya has a beautiful network of fine, white lines on its coat, against a rich chestnut background.

How do giraffes drink?

With necks as long as theirs it isn't easy! They have to spread their front legs first, and then lower the head and neck — otherwise it is quite impossible for them to reach the ground.

How tall can a giraffe grow?

An adult male (bull) giraffe can grow to around 5.5 metres (18 feet), sometimes even more. A new-born giraffe can often be about 1.8 metres (about six feet) tall! Adult females are usually between 60 and 90 centimetres shorter than adult males. In some zoos a scale is provided in the giraffes' enclosure so that visitors can measure the height of the animals for themselves.

Is it true that giraffes are mute?

Giraffes are certainly very silent creatures and it is rare to hear them make any sound at all. But giraffes can grunt and snort and some observers claim to have heard them make a noise like a roar!

What are their chief enemies?

Their great size means that adult giraffes have few, if any, natural enemies. A very young one may occasionally be attacked by lions or hyaenas. The adults are given a wide berth by such animals, since the giraffe can defend itself very effectively by using its strong legs and heavy hooves to kick out at an enemy. Giraffes are able to kick in all directions, with both front and back legs, and a sledgehammer blow from a giraffe's hoof may be lethal for another animal.

Giraffes sometimes slip while eating and get their heads stuck in the branches. When this happens they can die of strangulation or exhaustion from struggling. But this happens very, very rarely.

Is it true that giraffes never sit or lie down?

It is very unusual to see a giraffe sitting down in the wild. For one thing, because of its size and long legs, it takes a giraffe longer to stand up again than it does most other animals. A giraffe sitting down is also relatively defenceless and therefore more liable to be attacked. Giraffes in captivity, on the other hand, frequently sit down to rest, presumably because they have learnt that there are no dangers about.

How many horns does a giraffe have?

Most giraffes possess only two horns, but some races have another smaller pair growing behind the first. Adult bull giraffes also have a horny bump on the forehead, making a total of three or five horns. The horns are made of hollow bone surrounded by skin and hair. They only grow a few centimetres in length and are rather like a pair of velvety deer antlers.

Where is the okapi found?

The okapi is found only in the depths of the Ituri/Semliki forests of Zaire in central Africa, and there is only one species. It is a dark chocolate brown colour with a velvety coat and has horizontal white stripes on both front and back legs which help to disguise it as it moves about through the shadowy jungle.

Outside its natural habitat no one knew of its existence until 1901, when Sir Harry Johnston obtained some skulls and pieces of skin from the local pygmies. At first he thought it must be a kind of zebra, because of the stripes.

Is the okapi very different from the giraffe?

The okapi is the giraffe's only close relation, but it has a much shorter neck so it cannot reach anywhere like as high for its leafy food. Unlike the giraffe, it can only be found in dense forest, where it moves about silently and almost always alone.

Is the okapi rare?

The okapi is thought to be rare, but that may be because it is so solitary and can only be found in such a small area. The okapi has such a remarkable ability to blend with its surroundings that it is hardly ever seen. However, many okapi have been caught in traps, which suggests that the population is in fact quite high. A few can be seen in zoos and they breed in captivity quite successfully.

Camels and llamas, wild goats, sheep and pigs

I think that of all groups of animals, this particular one has the worst name for grubby members, especially the old pig and the rest of his family. I think that Martin Banks may well dispel that little bit of gossip — but read on and see for yourself.

By the way Miss Piggy told me last time we were speaking that she is no relative to the gentleman on page 83. In fact she says he's just an old 'bore'!

Rolf Harris

5

Camels and llamas belong to the family *Camelidae*. They differ from other even-toed ungulates in having more developed limbs, a stomach which is divided into three parts, and no side toes. They walk on the springy, horny soles of their feet. There are two species of camel, one found in Asia and the other in Africa and Arabia. Four species of llama exist, two in the wild and two domesticated. All four live in South America.

Sheep and goats are two closely related groups of hoofed mammals. They are found living in similar environments in several regions of the world, principally in Asia. There is a large number of different species, some of which are the ancestors of our domestic varieties.

Pigs are well known throughout the whole world. They are found in Europe, Africa, Asia and the Americas. Unlike most other even-toed ungulates, pigs are omnivorous (that is, they will eat almost anything), and their diet includes a great variety of animal and vegetable matter. They are also remarkable amongst hoofed mammals in producing large litters of young, rather than a single offspring at a time.

How many humps does the camel have?

The Bactrian camel, which is found principally in the cold desert regions of Asia, has two humps. It has a thick coat and is generally bigger than the Arabian camel, also called the dromedary, which has only one hump.

Are there any wild camels?

Camels of both kinds have been domesticated for hundreds of years. Until recently, it was thought that their wild ancestors had long been extinct. But is is now known that small numbers of Bactrian camels still live wild in the cold deserts of Mongolia. These are truly wild camels, as distinct from a number of Arabian camels which are found living 'wild' in countries such as Australia and southern Spain. These camels have escaped from man and run wild, but they are still domestic animals.

Bactrian camel

How do the wild Bactrian camels differ from their domestic relatives?

The wild camel is more slender than its domestic counterpart. It has a shorter coat and thinner fringes of hair on the neck and legs. Its ears are shorter and its hump and feet are smaller. Wild Bactrian camels live in small herds, usually led by an old male. They are swift runners and normally avoid contact with man, although they will mate with his domestic camels if the two happen to meet.

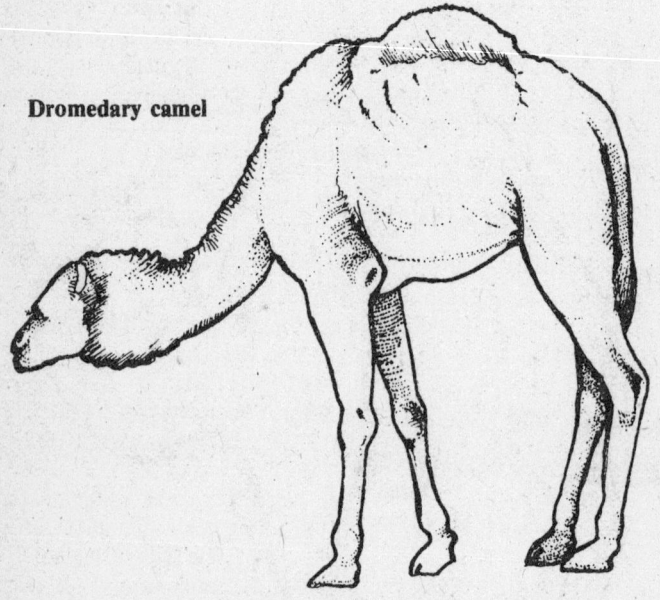

Dromedary camel

Which species is used for 'camel racing'?

Usually the Arabian camel or dromedary, which is a taller, more finely built animal than its two-humped Asian relative. Dromedaries used for racing are usually specially bred on the same lines as race horses. Thus a racing camel is usually faster and more streamlined than its more humble relatives which are used for everyday work in the desert.

Do camels store water in their humps?

No! Nor in their stomachs either. What they can do is drink large quantities of water in one go (many gallons in some cases), but this water is not retained by the camel for any length of time. What camels store in their humps is fat, which then reacts chemically inside the animal's body to produce water. Without water to drink *or* water produced by the fat in their humps, camels become dried out. This is why a camel in good condition has tall, firm humps. Camels drink whenever water is available to them, and although they can last several days without drinking if necessary, water is as vital to them as it is to other animals. Without it they soon die.

In what other ways are camels adapted to desert life?

The Bactrian camel lives in the colder deserts. It has thick fur to keep it warm, padded feet to cushion it against the rough ground, and nostrils which it can close completely in order to prevent windblown sand and grit getting up its nose! The Arabian species has long interlocking eyelashes to protect its eyes against the fierce sun and wind. It too has broad padded feet to allow it to move easily over soft sand and rocky ground. The Arabian camel has shorter fur than the Bactrian camel, because it lives in a much hotter environment. It can also regulate its body heat and moisture content so that it only begins to sweat at very high temperatures, thus conserving valuable moisture within its body.

Is it true that camels are bad-tempered?

Both species of camel *seem* to be rather haughty,

unfriendly creatures. They appear to take a dim view of working for man as beasts of burden. In fact, they are patient, hard-working creatures that can put up with conditions that would kill other animals — heat, drought, dust storms and lack of vegetation are all acceptable to the camel. Camels certainly don't have perfect manners: they can bite and spit, and often do so if displeased. When male camels come into breeding condition, they are particularly unpredictable and can be quite dangerous.

What sort of noises do camels make?

Camels are often silent for long periods of time, but they do make a variety of rather unpleasant noises. They groan, grunt and scream hideously, and also spit and roar! Most of the time this only happens when the animals are upset.

Which are the camel's nearest relatives?

The camels share the family *Camelidae* with four species of llama. The llamas look quite like the camels, with the important exception that they have no humps. Llamas are also considerably smaller.

Where do llamas live?

Llamas are confined to South America. The four species include two which are found only in a domestic state — one species confusingly just called the llama, and the other the alpaca — and two which still exist in the wild, the guanaco and the vicuna.

Which is the largest of the llama species?

The guanaco, which is gingerish in colour, is the tallest, measuring about 1.2 metres (four feet) at the shoulder and 1.8 metres (six feet) from the top of the head. The domestic llama is possibly bigger and heavier, but since it is stockier it is not quite as tall. The alpaca is shorter than the domestic llama. Smallest and most lightly built of the four is the vicuna.

Llama

Is the llama species descended from the guanaco or the vicuna?

It used to be thought that the llama was the domestic form of the guanaco, but now this appears not to be so. Llamas and guanacos appear to be different species, rather than merely wild and domestic forms of the same animal. It appears that the llama is descended from another species of wild llama which is now extinct.

How do these animals live?

The wild species are found living in open country, often at great altitude on plateau areas where the climate is cold. They are well protected from cold weather by a thick coverage of hair or wool. The guanaco and vicuna live in groups consisting of females and young each led by a male. Males without herds form bachelor groups. The herd males often act as sentries when their groups are feeding. They will jealously defend their group against rival males, or in the face of danger.

How do domestic llamas differ from the wild ones?

Llamas and alpacas are found living in large herds, the result of artificial husbandry by man. They have been selectively bred for their meat and wool, and no longer exhibit the clearly defined social groupings of the wild species. They have long woolly coats and can be either white or multi-coloured, it is most unlikely that their wild ancestors looked the same. Llamas are used as beasts of burden, like camels, but neither they nor the alpacas are ever ridden.

Are the wild llamas rare?

Both the guanaco and the vicuna are rare and in some danger of extinction. This particularly applies to the smaller vicuna, which is believed to possess the finest wool in the world for which it has been hunted mercilessly. Found at high altitudes in the Andes mountains, the vicuna seems less easy to domesticate than the other species. American Indians used to round them up for shearing, like sheep, but they always let them go afterwards. The vicunas surviving today are restricted to the remotest regions. Attempts have been made in recent years to save them. Small herds have been enclosed on large ranches within their existing habitat. Here they become fairly tame and breed quite well. But very few vicuna exist outside such areas, and those that do are still hunted.

What are the differences between wild goats and wild sheep?

Together, goats and sheep form a large group of animals which have some curious relations. There are some goat-like animals which represent halfway stages between antelopes and goats — the Himalayan gorals,

Wild goat

for example, are called 'goat antelopes'. Others are like a cross between sheep and antelopes, or as in the case of the musk oxen, between sheep and cattle. Broadly speaking, goats are mountain dwellers, with a beard under the chin and scent glands under the tail. Both sexes are horned, and the horns are ringed and sometimes arched or twisted. Goats are browsers whereas sheep are grazing animals. Female sheep are not always horned, and the horns of the males normally curve downwards.

Where are wild goats found?

True species of wild goat are found in Asia and Europe. Domestic goats, which claim several of the wild species among their ancestors, are found in nearly every country to the world. They are tough, hardy animals, adapted to almost any type of climate or terrain, and they can exist in even the poorest habitats. Herds of domestic goats can be very destructive to vegetation. Where domestic goats have gone wild, they become shy and wary and difficult to control.

Are there any wild goats in Britain?

So called wild goats are found in several parts of Britain, principally in remote mountainous areas in Wales, Scotland and the Lake District and on several off-shore islands around the coast. But all of them are 'feral' goats, descendants of domestic goats which have reverted to a wild type of life. These goats are often larger than their tame relatives, with thick coats of flowing hair. The males (or 'billies', as they are called) often carry impressive horns of great length and thickness.

What do goats eat?

Goats are browsing animals. They eat the leaves, bark, branches and twigs of a wide variety of bushes, trees and plants. In areas where there are no trees, they will eat grasses instead. This is why domestic goats in large numbers can have such a harmful effect on the countryside. When you see a goat tethered by the roadside, you may notice that it will eat vegetation from the hedge, before it starts on the grass.

Are there many species of wild goat?

One species occurs in a large area of middle-eastern Asia. This is thought to be the principal ancestor of the domestic goat. Another species, the markhor, is found in mountainous regions of eastern Asia. It has remarkable spiralled horns. The ibex occurs in a number of countries in Europe, Asia, Arabia and northern Africa. Each area has its own race of ibex. They are powerful, graceful animals which live most of the year at a dizzy height on the precipices and scree slopes of mountains. The males have huge, curving horns, which in some races may be over 91 centimetres (three feet) long. The Rocky Mountain goat of North America does not appear to be a true goat, but it is closely related. It is snow white and shaggy-coated for a life living on and above the snowline. The chamois of Europe and Asia is another mountain animal which is related to the goats.

Which is the rarest of the goats?

Several of these animals are rare. Of the true goats, the ibex is possibly the rarest. Although it has several races, some of these — such as the Spanish ibex — are in danger of extinction. Rarest of all is probably the very fine Walia ibex, which is found only in the high mountains of Ethiopia.

Where are wild sheep found?

Wild sheep have much the same habitat as the wild goats. They are found in rocky terrain and in mountains, where they move about with great agility and surefootedness on the narrow ledges. They are found chiefly in central and southern Asia. Unlike goats, sheep have a flattened forehead and facial glands. Their tails, on the other hand, are not flattened, and during the mating season the males lack the powerful smell characteristic of goats.

Mouflon sheep

Are there any wild sheep living in Britain?

The breeds of sheep which are found in many upland areas of Britain, such as the moorlands of Wales, Scotland and the west of England are certainly wild in contrast to the fat and fleecy sheep of the lowlands. But they are merely breeds of domestic sheep which are better equipped to live in a harsher environment. All of them are owned by farmers and they are periodically rounded up for inspection, sale or shearing. In hard winters they need artificial feeding if they are to remain fit and healthy. Soay sheep, a breed found only on the St Kilda group of islands in the Inner Hebrides, are far more primitive. But even they are thought to be a primitive form of domestic sheep which were brought to this country by invading Norsemen, hundreds of years ago. Here they have remained, unchanged and untamed, and they are the nearest thing we have to a truly wild species of sheep in Britain.

Are wild sheep similar in appearance to the domestic varieties?

While some of the wild species are the ancestors of domestic sheep, there is not much similarity between them. Wild sheep are usually short-haired (the thick fleece of domestic sheep has been selectively bred by man). Wild sheep are hardy and cunning, unlike the domestic varieties which appear to be relatively docile. The species of wild sheep most commonly seen in captivity is the smaller mouflon.

Do wild sheep live in large flocks?

Wild sheep are normally found in small groups, which consist either of females and their young, or of adult males. The males only associate with the females at breeding time, when they challenge and fight each other for possession of the female groups. This is the time when males square up to each other, rise on their hind legs and clash their heads together again and again, in order to establish dominance. At other times of the year, these males live peaceably together in bachelor groups.

What are the correct names for male, female and young goats and sheep?

Male goats are known as 'billies', the females as 'nannies' and the young as 'kids'. Male sheep are called 'rams', the females 'ewes' and the young 'lambs'. These names apply to the wild species as well as to the domestic ones.

Where are wild pigs found?

Wild pigs of various species are found in nearly all parts of the world, except Australia. The pigs of the Americas — called peccaries — are not closely related to the pigs of other countries, although they look quite similar. They have their own family, the *Tayassuidae,* while the other pigs belong to the family *Suidae.*

What is the ancestor of the domestic pig?

The wild boar, which is a species of wild pig, is generally regarded as being the ancestor of domestic pigs. It is found in Europe, and across Asia to China, and extends from the far north to the jungles of India and south-east Asia. It used to be found in Britain too, but was exterminated here by the beginning of the eighteenth century. Many different races exist, but they differ only in size and other minor points. Centuries of domestication have given us the heavy, long-bodied, lop-eared pig we all know. Now it is difficult to imagine that the powerful, muscular and long-snouted wild boar is the ancestor of our domestic pig.

Are wild boars dangerous?

The wild boar holds a special place in the tales and folklore of hunters. When boars are hunted, as they are in many parts of their territory, they can prove dangerous, especially when cornered and injured. At such times they can charge like lightning, and are quick to defend themselves with their sharp tusks. They can inflict nasty wounds and have occasionally killed people. But when left alone, they are peaceable creatures, and seek only to avoid man.

Wild boar

What is their natural habitat?

Wild boar are essentially forest animals. They prefer mixed forest of deciduous trees, as these hold the greatest variety of food. The wild boar's diet consists largley of bulbs, fruits, roots, small animals — in fact almost anything edible. In some areas they live in marshes or dense scrub, from which they emerge in the evening to forage for food in the surrounding countryside.

How many young do the various sorts of pig have?

Most species of wild pig have litters of piglets numbering from three to eight at a time. The wild boar constructs a nest in which to give birth to its young. Young African warthogs live in burrows while they are small. Peccaries normally give birth to only one, two or three young at a time. The really large litters of piglets which domestic pigs commonly produce are the result of domestication and selective breeding.

Are pigs really dirty and lazy?

From the way many pigs are kept on farms, it often appears that they relish spending the day wallowing in mud and muck. Wild pigs, and domestic ones, too, when they are given the chance, are extremely clean animals. Wild pigs are alert, active and agile and are also cunning at detecting and avoiding danger. Most pigs swim well and enjoy wallowing in mud. This is not because they are lazy: the mud helps to keep them cool and softens their coarse skin. Most pigs are semi-nocturnal, resting during the main part of the day and foraging chiefly from dusk until dawn.

Are hedgehogs related to pigs?

The only similarity between hedgehogs and pigs is in their name. Hedgehogs are insect-eating creatures which bear no relation to pigs.

How do pigs avoid danger?

Pigs have an excellent sense of smell. Their hearing is moderately good, and their eyesight relatively poor in contrast to their other senses. They rely on smell and hearing to detect danger, and a quick dash to cover in order to avoid it. When frightened, a group of pigs usually scatter, and regroup again after the danger has passed. Adult wild pigs, in particular the boars, have formidable teeth. If cornered by a predator, they often try to fight their way out. Quite often their sharp teeth and aggressive behaviour serve them very well and allow them to escape.

Do pigs live singly, in pairs or in groups?

This depends on the species. Some forest species, such as the giant forest hog and the red river hog of Africa are normally found either singly or in twos and threes. Wild boars usually occur in groups of males, females and young, known as 'sounders'. The largest and oldest boars often live a solitary existence for most of the time. In contrast the collared peccary of the Americas is often found in herds of up to a hundred individuals.

Are any of the pigs very rare?

The babirussa is found only in Celebes and adjacent islands. In this species, one pair of tusks in the adult male actually grows through holes in the skin of the upper jaw, while a second pair grows out from below it. This 'pig with four tusks' is found in forested areas and may be very rare; certainly, little is known about it. The giant forest hog of central and east Africa is another rarely seen animal whose numbers are unknown. At the other end of the scale, the tiny pigmy hog of the Himalayan foothills was only rediscovered quite recently, after being considered extinct. It may be relatively common within a very limited area.

The big cats

Cats — I'm unashamedly mad about them. At home we have seven of the smaller kind — Fluffy Breeches, Cloudy, Weed, Mole, Purrsha, Smudge and Ratbag. Therefore one of the nicest things about being involved with this book was being taken on a trip to a wildlife park and meeting our young friend on the cover. Mind you, his mother, though just as lovely, was not quite as cuddly, if you see what I mean . . .

Rolf Harris

6

Probably no other animals are more respected and admired than the fierce and noble larger members of the cat family. The lion is popularly known as 'King of the Beasts', and the beautiful striped tiger is truly 'Lord of the Jungle' wherever he is still found. Amongst the most skilful hunters are the graceful and stealthy spotted cats; the leopard of Africa and Asia and the jaguar of South America. In the mountains of the Himalayas lives the very rare and beautiful snow leopard. Somewhat apart from the other big cats is the cheetah, the graceful sprinter of the African plains. Although it shares many of the characteristics of the other big cats, it is in other ways rather more like a dog!

As well as the big cats, there is a variety of medium-sized and smaller wild cats, many of which are spotted or striped. Although most of these are outside the scope of this chapter, one, the lynx, is worth mentioning. Although it is a medium-sized cat, it is the largest member of the family still to be found in Europe.

Which is the larger of the big cats, the lion or the tiger?

Tigers are found in several different sizes. The biggest ones come from Manchuria and Siberia. They are larger than any lion and may measure 3.66 metres (12 feet) in length as against 2.74 metres (9 feet) or 3.04 metres (10 feet) for a lion. The Indian tiger and the lion are about the same size, while the Javan and the Sumatran races of tiger are smaller than the average lion.

Are lions found only in Africa?

Today, the only lions existing outside Africa are a small population in the Gir forest of north-west India. Here some 200-300 lions are found living in a forest of thorn scrub. A second reserve for the Indian lion has been created recently, but the animals had to be introduced from the Gir forest. Lions were once found over a wide area of southern Asia, as well as over a much larger area of Africa than at present. In biblical times, they still existed in Europe and Syria. Today they are extinct in all these countries, except Africa and India.

Which sort are seen in zoos and circuses?

African lions breed very freely in captivity. Many have lived in captive surroundings for generations, and the lions used for stocking new zoos or wildlife parks are nearly always obtained from other zoos which have bred them. This is far more economical than importing them from Africa. Indian lions are only to be seen in a very few zoos outside India, chiefly because they are rare and difficult to obtain.

What are the differences between African and Indian lions?

The differences are very slight. The African lion is often said to have a heavier mane. The Indian lion has a thick tuft of hair at the tip of its tail and thick fringes of hair on its belly and on the elbows of its front legs. Apart from this, the two races of lion are very similar and of almost identical size.

Why do male lions have manes?

The mane of the male lion provides a puzzle. It may be

African lion

simply a form of protective covering, but no other big cats grow manes, nor do female lions; even some male lions don't have them. In the wild, a male lion's mane starts to grow when the animal is approaching two years of age. It is kept in check as the lion rubs against vegetation as he moves through the bush. In captivity, lions often grow very thick, luxurious manes.

Are lions' manes always the same colour?

Some lions have blonde manes, others have black manes. Many lions have tawny or ginger-coloured manes. The colour seems to vary from area to area although, in some places, lions with several different mane colours can be seen together. In the past, some races of lion which are now extinct were identified by mane colour. Even today, some parts of east Africa are well known for their black-maned lions.

How do lions live in the wild?

A social group of lions is known as a pride. Each pride numbers between 5 and 20 lions on average. The pride consists of several adult lionesses and their cubs of various ages. It is normally headed by one or more adult males. This form of social grouping is unusual among the normally solitary cat family, but not all lions live in prides. A number of adult males, and also some lionesses, live a nomadic life, wandering in ones and twos across the plains. They are not attached to any pride and are often unwelcome if they stray into a pride's territory. Nomad males and pride males sometimes swap leadership, usually after some fighting.

Which lion is head of the pride?

Pride life is normally governed by the eldest females. Although there are usually one or more splendid males in attendance, they sometimes move from one pride to another, or leave to become nomads. The adult lionesses on the other hand, often remain together for many years and it is they who form the backbone of the pride.

Is it true that the lionesses do all the hunting?

Lionesses do hunt a lot more often than adult males. But all lions over the age of two years are able to hunt for themselves. Males not attached to prides must do so regularly if they are not to go hungry. Within a pride, several lionesses often form a team when they hunt, and ambush their prey after stalking and surrounding it. But lionesses also hunt successfully alone.

Is it true that male lions always feed first at a kill?

Normally, the adult males of a pride feed first, even if they have taken no part in the hunt itself. They drive the lionesses and younger animals away and keep them at bay until their own hunger is blunted; they may tolerate lesser members of the pride eating with them. Even a small cub may be dealt a punishing blow or bite if it dares to approach too close to its superiors at feeding time. The order is; adult males first, then lionesses and lastly cubs and younger animals.

Does this mean that lions are poor parents?

Parental care in lions seems to depend on the available food supply. Lionesses are good mothers, but cubs occasionally get lost or are killed by male lions or strange females. When food is plentiful, the young cubs get their fair share of meat, even if they have to wait to eat it. When game is scarce, a lot of the young cubs simply die of starvation.

How many cubs are born in a litter?

Lionesses normally produce between two and four cubs in a litter. They are introduced to the mother's pride when they are able to walk. Before this the mother hides them away in the bush. Normally, two or three cubs in a litter survive.

Which animals does the lion hunt?

Zebras, buffaloes, wildebeest and large and medium-sized antelope form the major portion of the African lion's diet. They occasionally attack young or sick giraffes, and young rhinos, and they will also eat smaller mammals and birds, and steal the remains of other predators' kills. The Indian lion's natural diet is chiefly medium-sized deer and antelope, and wild boar. But in the Gir forest only wild boar are common, and the lions prey on the cattle of local villagers in order to obtain sufficient food.

How many species of tiger are there?

All tigers belong to a single species, of which the Indian tiger is the typical example. But several different races exist and these differ in size and in the colour and pattern of their coats. The large Siberian tiger of Siberia and Manchuria is the largest and palest of all the tigers. The other races are the Indian, the Caspian (now probably extinct) and the smaller Javan and Sumatran tigers. The sixth race, the Bali tiger, is now almost certainly extinct. This was the smallest and most southerly race.

Which is the smallest tiger?

After the Balinese tiger, the rare Javan and Sumatran races are the smallest. Adults of these races are roughly two-thirds the size of an adult Siberian tiger.

Which is the rarest tiger?

All tigers are extremely rare and in danger of extinction. In the past they were hunted as trophies — it was a great

Indian tiger

distinction simply to have caught one. Today, despite protection, they are illegally hunted for their skins. In addition, the forests in which they live are being cut down at an alarming rate. The Indian tiger still numbers a few thousand individuals, but many of these are not living in protected reserves. At the last count, there were only some five or six Javan tigers left, and the Caspian tiger is not definitely known to exist at all any more.

Which tigers are most commonly seen in captivity?

The Indian tiger is the race most commonly seen in zoos, and normally the only one exhibited in circuses. Some zoos and wildlife parks also keep the large Siberian tiger, and a few have the Sumatran tiger (which is smaller and darker). In the past, tigers of different races were crossed indiscriminately, but nowadays records are kept to ensure that the races are kept pure wherever possible.

Do tigers breed freely in captivity?

Some collections have a very good record for breeding tigers but, on the whole, tigers do not breed in captivity as freely as lions. In the past this may have been due to unsuitable conditions, since tigers are nervous creatures which need quiet and solitude for the successful raising of their cubs.

What are 'white' tigers?

White tigers are a mutation of the Indian tiger, which in recent years has been selectively bred in captivity. They are creamy white with dark brown stripes, pink paws and blue eyes. They have occurred from time to time in the Indian jungles and most of those currently living in captivity are descended from a male of this type which was captured in 1951. Animals of such freak colour are unlikely to survive in the wild for long. Pure white tigers (lacking pigment and therefore called 'albinos') have only been recorded once, in India in the last century.

What turns a tiger into a man-eater?

Normally, tigers are shy creatures that avoid encounters with man. But just occasionally a tiger turns man-eater, or eats cattle. This normally happens only when a tiger either becomes too old to kill its normal prey efficiently, or has been prevented from doing so by an injury. The starving animal may then discover, perhaps by a chance encounter, that man is a slow, defenceless animal. Once the first, easy kill has been made, the tiger may seek out people to kill and eat again and again. A man-eating tiger often becomes famous locally, for nobody is safe until it has been killed. It is estimated that only three tigers in every thousand become man-eaters. Lions and leopards also sometimes exhibit this behaviour.

Are tigers sociable or solitary?

Tigers are essentially solitary creatures. Male and female only associate closely at mating time. But each male tiger occupies a large territory which may overlap with that of two or more tigresses. Sometimes two or three tigers will share the kill of one of them, without any quarrelling. The cubs, normally from one to four in a litter, remain with their mother until they are nearly two years old. During this time their mother teaches them all the skills of hunting which they will need to survive on their own. By the time they leave her to find territories of their own, the cubs are nearly full-sized.

Is it true that tigers like water?

Unlike most big cats, tigers spend a lot of time in the water. Most active at night, tigers in tropical countries often spend the hottest hours of the day keeping cool by lying in water, often up to their necks. They also swim freely and show every sign of enjoying the water.

Will a tiger breed with a lion?

The only place where wild tigers and lions are found living in the same country is in India. Even there, they are found in very different areas, and never meet naturally. But in captivity, lions and tigers have been crossed. The hybrid offspring are called 'tigons' or 'ligers'! They vary in appearance, but most of them resemble lions, often with faint spots and stripes on the body. The males often have a ruff of hair framing the face, which is characteristic of male tigers.

Where are leopards found?

Leopards are found in Africa, India and south-east Asia. There are also some in China and a few in Iran and Turkey. One was photographed in Palestine in 1975, the first recorded there for many years.

What animals do leopards eat?

Leopards feed on a variety of medium-sized hoofed animals, such as antelope, deer and wild pigs. They also take monkeys and baboons, and birds. Leopards in some areas show a remarkable liking for villagers' dogs, while domestic goats and other stock are also sometimes taken.

Why do leopards often store their uneaten kills in trees?

Leopards are solitary creatures and no match for a pack of marauding hyaenas or wild dogs or lions which may wish to steal a kill from them. So they frequently carry the remains of a large kill, such as an antelope, high up into a tree where other animals cannot reach it.

Snow leopard

How many species of leopard are there?

Although leopards in different countries belong to a single species, several different races occur, which, like the tiger, differ in size, colour and markings. The snow leopard of the Himalayas and the clouded leopard of south-eastern Asia are entirely different species.

What is a black panther?

A black panther is merely a black form of the ordinary spotted leopard. Black leopards (or panthers) are in no way different from ordinary leopards except in colour. The two types inter-breed freely, and young of both colours may sometimes be found in one litter. Black leopards are fairly common in south-east Asia, but rarer in Africa and India. They have a reputation for being fierce, but it is debatable if they are any fiercer than their paler relatives.

What is the difference between leopards and jaguars?

The leopard is more slender and more gracefully proportioned, with a small, neat head and a long, tapering tail. Its spots, which are distributed all over the body, are small 'rosettes'. By contrast, the jaguar looks clumsy. Although similar in overall size to the leopard, it has a heavy head, a chunky body and a thicker, shorter tail. However, although it is less graceful than the leopard, the jaguar has an even more beautiful pattern of markings. Its spots are larger and each spot has a light coloured area in its centre. Jaguars, like tigers, swim and play freely in the water, whereas leopards avoid water except for drinking. Like black leopards there are also some, if not many, black jaguars.

How do jaguars live?

Jaguars are confined to the jungles of tropical South America. They have similar habits to leopards, being nocturnal hunters of medium-sized animals such as peccaries and large South American rodents called capybaras. They also take birds and fish. Both leopards and jaguars are excellent climbers, although the leopard is the more agile. Jaguars are solitary animals. They communicate with each other by scent, and by roaring — a harsh coughing noise like the rasping of a saw. Leopards also have a similar call.

How do cheetahs differ from the other big cats?

Cheetahs are the greyhounds of the big cat family. In some ways they resemble dogs more than cats. For example, a cheetah's claws cannot be retracted or sheathed, unlike those of the other cats. Cheetahs can also be tamed and trained easily, since they are rather more docile than the other cats. The cheetah has a small head and rather weak jaws for a cat of its size. The length of its legs gives it great speed, but means that the cheetah is a poor climber of trees.

Are cheetahs the fastest of all land mammals?

Cheetahs have been known to move at up to 60 miles per hour, and claims have been made of up to 70 miles per hour. This does indeed make them the fastest of all land mammals. A cheetah can only sprint at this speed for a very short while when chasing prey. If they fail to catch up with their quarry quickly, they become tired and give up the hunt.

Cheetah

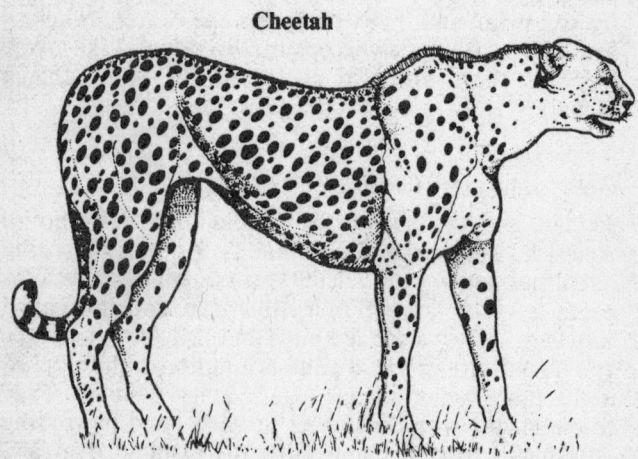

How do cheetahs catch their quarry?

Cheetahs usually start a hunt by scanning the plain for likely game, often from a vantage point such as an anthill or hillock. Having selected their quarry, they stalk to within a few hundred metres and then make a surprise dash, ending with a chase which rarely lasts for more than half a minute. If the cheetah catches up with its prey, it usually trips the running animal with its front claws, and thus bringing the animal to the ground. Cheetahs are so fast that they can catch even the fastest of the small and medium-sized antelope, but they also catch and kill smaller animals and young antelope.

Are cheetahs rare?

Cheetahs are becoming increasingly rare on the plains of east Africa. They are shy, nervous creatures that appear to require a lot of space, peace and quiet if they are to live and breed normally. Despite having been tamed and trained for hundreds of years, it is only in the last 20 years that Cheetahs have been successfully bred in captivity. Outside Africa, cheetahs used to be found in central Asia and in India, but the Indian cheetah is now extinct and only a very small number still exist in Iran.

Are cheetahs social animals?

Cheetahs tend to live solitary lives, with the exception of a mother growing cubs while she is teaching them the skills of hunting. Male and female cheetahs only appear to consort together at mating time, when two or more males may court one female. Cheetah cubs are likely to be preyed on by hyaenas and jackals, so the mother tries to keep them hidden. Adult cheetahs are no match for lions and hyaenas, and try to avoid them as much as possible. When a cheetah makes a kill, it normally drags it to cover before starting to eat it and then covers the remains in order to stop other animals discovering them.

What is an 'ounce'?

'Ounce' is another name for the snow leopard, which lives in small numbers in the Himalayas. The snow leopard has a long shaggy coat and a beautiful pattern of grey markings on a whitish background. It is now very rare.

What is a 'cougar'?

'Cougar' is an alternative name for the puma. It has several other names, including mountain lion, panther, painter and silver lion. Several races can be found, in North America and through central America into the northern part of South America. The pumas in the north of this large range are larger and greyish, those in the south smaller and reddish-brown.

What do pumas eat?

Pumas rely on stealth and surprise to catch their prey, which are chiefly medium-sized deer. South American pumas also take peccaries and the occasional capybara. Where pumas live near man, they are often responsible for taking domestic stock such as sheep and cattle. A full-grown puma is capable of carrying away a large calf! Understandably, pumas are unpopular with farmers, and are still hunted in some areas.

Are there any big cats found in Britain or Europe?

Although lions once lived in Europe, the nearest big cats are now the few leopards still found in the Middle East. In Europe, the largest surviving wild cat is the lynx. It is confined to forested regions, chiefly in Scandinavia and eastern Europe, while the lynx in Spain is a smaller, heavily spotted animal. The only wild cat found in Britain is the Scottish wildcat, about the size of a large domestic cat.

Bears, wolves and wild dogs

Well, we may not be covering the antics of the kangaroo in this book, but this chapter does include another famous Australian, that's the dingo. Furthermore, if you think that a polar bear does nothing but stand around on mints talking to a fox all day, Martin Banks is about to put you straight on that one.

Rolf Harris

7

All these animals eat meat. In many ways, bears are rather like overgrown dogs, although they walk in a different fashion and have very short tails. Bears are found in the Americas, Europe and Asia, but not in Africa or Australia. There are several different species. All bears give birth to a small number of young; in several species, these are born in a very undeveloped state in the course of the mother's long winter sleep (or hibernation). Wolves and wild dogs are found in many parts of the world, but the various species differ from each other quite distinctly. Like domestic dogs, wolves and most species of wild dog produce several young at a time, although never as many as domestic dogs.

Which is the largest of the bears?

The largest of all is found on Kodiak Island in the gulf of Alaska. These bears are a race of the American grizzly bear and, since they are larger than any of the big cats, they are the largest of all carnivorous (meat-eating) land animals. Large male polar bears are just slightly smaller.

Is it true that bears hibernate?

Bears that live in cold regions such as Asia and North America usually go into a deep sleep during the cold winter months. In the autumn each bear digs a sheltered den into which it retires for several months of sleep.

Kodiak Island grizzly bears

How does a bear survive during this period?

The thick coat of hair protects the bear from the cold, as does its own body heat in the confined space of the den. Because they expend so little energy during this time, bears are able to live off the fat reserves which they have built up during rich feeding in the autumn — but they are usually very hungry when they wake up again in the spring!

Do bears really eat porridge?

Most bears eat a wide variety of foods, including meat, fish, berries, fruits and grasses. In some national parks in North America and Canada, the bears have learned to beg for food from passing tourists, and they also raid campsites and rubbish tips for food. Bears in captivity are usually fed on meat, brown bread and fruit and vegetables. If they were offered porridge, they would no doubt make short work of it!

Why are polar bears white?

Polar bears are white so that they can blend in with their surroundings, the snow and ice of the frozen North. Polar bears hunt seals, and they can catch them more easily when they can approach them over the ice without being noticed.

Is it true that a polar bear hunting a seal covers its nose with its paw, to hide the black colour?

Polar bears are cunning animals but it seems unlikely that they are able to realise that a black nose stands out against a white background. When hunting, a polar bear often waits by the breathing hole of a seal in the ice and then pounces as the seal comes up to breathe, before it has a chance to look around.

Do all bears swim?

Polar bears are the best swimmers among the bears. Sometimes they are seen swimming strongly hundreds of kilometres from the nearest land. Brown bears also like water to bathe in, and in some areas they swim into the river to catch fish. Some of the other bears are less fond of water and do not enter it so regularly.

How many cubs are born in a litter?

Most species of bear normally give birth to between one and three cubs in a litter. Two is a common number. At birth, the cubs are very tiny and undeveloped. A newborn brown or polar bear is scarcely bigger than a large rat. The cubs develop slowly at first and remain with their mother for a year or more while they are growing up.

Is the male bear a good father?

Male bears play no part in family life. After mating, the female retires to a den to have her cubs, and she avoids meeting a male while her cubs are still with her. Male bears occasionally kill young cubs if they meet them in their travels.

Which is the smallest bear?

The Malayan sun bear is the smallest of the bears. It is found in forested areas of south-east Asia. An adult sun bear is only about 91 centimetres (three feet) long and stands only about 61 centimetres (two feet) high at the shoulder. Sun bears have black, glossy coats with a yellow patch under the throat. They feed on fruits and small animals and make nests in trees. They are also known to be fond of honey, which they obtain by raiding bees' nests. Perhaps they are responsible for the tale that all bears love honey, which is true for most species.

Which is the rarest of the bears?

Rarest of the true bears is undoubtedly the spectacled bear, the only species found in South America. Several other species, such as the polar bear, the sloth bear of India and the European brown bear are also in some danger of extinction.

Is the giant panda a true bear?

The rare giant panda is not regarded as being a true bear. Most zoologists now think it is more closely related to the racoon family, and that it only resembles bears in its appearance. Its remarkable colours, its diet of bamboo shoots, and the structure of its skull and teeth all set it apart from real bears. In addition, the giant panda has extra 'thumbs' on its front feet which enable it to grip and hold things 'single-handed' —

something which other bears cannot do.

Are bears dangerous?

All bears can be dangerous if molested or injured. The polar and North American grizzly bears have a particular reputation for cunning and fierceness. Most bears only want to be left alone, but if they bump into someone by surprise they may attack instead of retreating. Some American black bears wander into picnic sites and can become aggressive if food is withheld from them.

Can bears really hug people to death?

The term 'bear hug' is used to describe a very tight squeeze. Presumably it is thought that bears can use this method to kill other animals, and perhaps people. Bears usually attack by biting with their teeth and slashing with their long claws.

Have bears ever lived in Britain?

Yes, but the brown bear that lived in Britain died out ten centuries ago. There are still a few of them in Spain and Italy, and larger numbers in eastern Europe and Russia.

Where are wolves found in the wild?

Wolves are found in North America and Canada and across Asia from western Europe to China. They are also found in south-east Asia and India, but not in Africa.

How many species of wolf are there?

The North American timber wolf and the wolf of Europe and Asia are really the same species, although wolves in different countries differ in size, colour and habitat. In North America, a second species, the red wolf, lives in Texas, but it is now very rare. The maned wolf of South America is a very different animal which, despite its large size, is more closely related to foxes than to wolves.

Were wolves once found in Britain?

Wolves were once found in many parts of the British Isles, but they were exterminated because they were regarded as a dangerous menace. Wolves can still be found in small numbers in some European countries such as Spain and Italy.

European wolf

What are werewolves?

These are mythical creatures, supposed to be half-man, half-wolf. Although they are popular in folklore and horror stories, there is no evidence that such animals ever existed.

Is it true that wolves have reared human children together with their own pups?

This is a popular theory. Romulus and Remus, the twins who founded Rome, were supposed to have been reared by a wolf. Mowgli, in Rudyard Kipling's *Jungle Book,* was another 'wolf-child'. Even today, reports sometimes come in of children who have been discovered living wild in the jungles of India. They are said to walk on all fours, eat meat and be unable to speak. But it seems very unlikely that they have really been reared by a wolf.

Why do wolves hunt in packs?

Wolves usually hunt in packs to enable them to pull down large animals, such as deer. They normally only hunt in packs during the winter. During spring and summer, wolves live and hunt in pairs, feeding on a variety of smaller animals that are easy to find at this time of year. A wolf pack rarely contains more than a dozen or so animals, and usually comprises one or more family groups. Within the pack, each wolf has its own rank and normally only the top-ranking male and female in each pack will breed.

Why do wolves howl?

Wolves howl as a means of communication to other wolves within earshot and possibly also to show their presence in a territory. Wolves can also bark like dogs (and dogs can howl like wolves). Wolves use a variety of expressions and movements to show their feelings and moods to other wolves in the pack.

Why are wolves hunted?

In the countries where wolves are still found, they are often regarded as pests, because they kill domestic animals such as sheep and cattle. In some places, they are also thought to reduce the numbers of wild game. Now some countries are protecting their wolves, which in some places have almost been wiped out.

Which animals do wolves prey on?

Wolves kill deer in large numbers. Wild pigs and antelope are also eaten. In summer, large numbers of smaller animals are eaten, such as rabbits, mice, young deer and birds.

Are dogs descended from wolves?

Wolves are usually thought to be the ancestors of domestic dogs, but some people believe that jackals are the true ancestors. It may be that some breeds of dog are descended from wolves, and others from the jackal. Alternatively, the wild ancestor of our domestic dogs might be a now-extinct species of wild dog.

Can wolves be tamed?

Wolves can be tamed, if they are taken as young puppies and brought up with close human contact. Sometimes they can even be trained to understand and obey commands in the same way as dogs although, being wild animals by nature, they do not take so easily to training. Probably the very first dogs which prehistoric man kept were puppies of wild dogs or wolves which he raised and tamed in this fashion.

Are Alsatians more closely related to wolves than most other dogs?

All dogs, whatever their breed or appearance, have been domesticated for thousands of years, although new breeds are sometimes created from existing ones. Alsatians are no more closely related to wolves than are spaniels or poodles. Only in their outward appearance are they something like a wolf.

What are coyotes?

Coyotes are found in North America. They look very like wolves but are a lot smaller. They are normally found singly or in pairs and do not hunt in packs. Whereas wolves have been hunted to extinction in some parts of North America, the coyote, equally regarded a pest seems to be as common as ever.

How many species of wild dog are there?

The term 'wild dog' is a very general one and covers various different species, not all of which are very closely related, found in many different countries. The hunting dog of Africa and the dhole of India and Asia are among them. There are three species of jackal. The maned wolf, which looks like a large fox on stilts, and is found in South America, is another. Also in South America another very different creature, the small and ugly bush dog, is found.

What is a dingo?

The dingo seems to be a very primitive form of domestic dog, rather than a truly wild species. It was introduced to Australia a very long time ago. Dingoes are now considered a great pest in Australia, where they live a wild existence and are very cunning. The dingo is smooth-haired and sandy-coloured. It is about the size of a collie dog.

What are 'pariah' dogs?

Pariah dogs are similar to dingoes in appearance. They are ordinary domestic dogs of no fixed breed which live a semi-wild existence around villages and settlements in many tropical parts of the world. They exist rather like the stray dogs which are sometimes found in other parts of the world, except that they are taken for granted and never rounded up.

African hunting dogs (mother and pup)

Do wild dogs form packs?

Wild dogs which live and hunt in packs include the African hunting dog and the Asian dhole. Both these species rely on endurance in tracking and following their chosen quarry until it becomes exhausted and they can catch up with it. The jackals of Africa and Asia and the

American coyote are chiefly scavengers, feeding on the kills of big cats. They also catch small animals themselves. They usually live singly or in pairs, since they do not need 'team' effort to obtain food.

Which is the rarest of the wild dogs?

The Simien fox. This is a species related to the jackals, and found only in the mountains of Ethiopia in northeast Africa, where a few hundred exist. The extraordinary maned wolf of South America is also in danger of extinction. This unusual creature feeds on small mammals such as mice, and is thought to eat at least as much fruit and vegetable matter as it does meat.

Are hyaenas related to dogs?

Only distantly. In some respects, hyaenas appear to be more closely related to the big cats than to dogs.

How many species of hyaena are there?

Three species of hyaena exist — the spotted, the striped and the brown. The spotted hyaena of Africa is the species most frequently seen in captivity.

Are hyaenas scavengers?

Hyaenas lead a sort of Jekyll and Hyde existence! By day they are frequently seen crunching up the remains of a lion's kill. But at night the spotted hyaena hunts in packs, and a good percentage of its food is caught, not scavenged from other predators. This has only recently been discovered.

Do hyaenas really laugh?

Hyaenas make a wide variety of noises, best known of which is the strange series of high-pitched yelps which to us sounds like laughter. But the hyaena uses this noise to show excitement or as a call to other hyaenas, not because it is amused.

Are hyaenas really cowardly?

Hyaenas have an unfortunate appearance, because their forequarters are taller than their hindquarters which always makes them look furtive and slinking. In fact, a large group of hyaenas can drive a small pride of lions from a kill. They have very strong teeth and jaws, which are capable of cracking and breaking up even the strongest bones.

What are the main enemies of these animals?

Bears, wolves and wild dogs are all carnivorous animals which are at the top of the food chain. In other words, nothing else eats or preys on them. Jackals and some of the other smaller wild dogs may occasionally get killed by a leopard or a lion which is feeding at a kill, but they are normally very careful to keep their distance until a larger predator has finished feeding, before moving in to pick off the remains.

Man is the only real enemy of bears and wolves. Unfortunately, in some areas he has been a very real enemy and has drastically reduced the numbers of both.

Apes, monkeys and lemurs

Finally we move onto the monkey business — as everyone who has seen them will know, these cheeky fellows are the comedians of the mammal world. Martin Banks and I introduced this book by pointing out that man was in fact a mammal — well here is man's closest relative in the animal world. And a hairy bunch of relatives they are too!

Rolf Harris

8

These animals belong to the order of primates, which includes man. The three great apes — the gorilla, chimpanzee and orangutan — are man's nearest relatives. The gibbon is also considered to be an ape as it is tail-less, although it is smaller and more monkey-like than the other apes.

Gorillas and chimpanzees live in forests in Africa. Both spend much of their time on the ground, although the chimpanzee in particular is a good tree climber. The orangutan and the gibbon are found in Asia. They live almost entirely in the trees.

Monkeys are smaller than apes, and most of them have tails. There are many species of monkey, but there is a simple division between the monkeys of the Old World (Africa and Asia) and the monkeys of the New World (South America). Many of the South American monkeys can use their tails as a fifth limb. This is not possible for any of the Old World monkeys.

Lemurs are the simplest and most primitive of primates. They are now found only on the island of Madagascar and a few nearby islands. They lack the 'human' appearance of the other primates, but are found in a wide variety of shapes and sizes.

Which is the largest of all the apes and monkeys?

The three great apes are all larger than any of the monkeys. The gorilla is the largest of these, with the orangutan in second place and the chimpanzee third.

Male gorilla

How many species of gorilla are there?

There is only one species of gorilla, and it lives in the forests of west and central Africa. The gorillas in central Africa are slightly larger and shaggier and live high up on forested mountain slopes. The gorillas of west Africa are known as lowland gorillas, the two types being races of the same animal.

Are gorillas really fearsome terrors of the jungle?

Gorillas used to be thought of as raging giants, crashing through the jungle tearing down trees and anybody who dared stand in their path. Now we know that these large apes, which share many similarities with ourselves, are timid, peaceful creatures. They are quite harmless if left alone and feed only on the leaves and fruits of plants.

How do gorillas live in the wild?

Gorillas are always found living in family groups. Each group is led by a strong adult male (known as a 'silverback' from the colour of the hair on his back). His group includes several females and young, and perhaps one or more other adult or younger males. The group moves daily within an area of jungle, although there is no fixed territory. The day is spent feeding, travelling and resting by turn and the animals build crude nests in which to sleep at night. Some adult males live solitary lives for several months at a time, but may then rejoin another group.

Do they build their nests in the trees?

Although gorillas can climb trees, the adults are too heavy to climb freely. The nests, which are made of weeds and plant stems, are built on the ground. New nests are normally built each night at dusk, wherever the group happens to be. Each member sits and just pulls in the stalks and stems within reach to make a rough nest. Occasionally young gorillas will build a nest off the ground in a tree or bush.

Do gorillas pound their chests?

Yes, but not for the reasons we think. They don't do it only as a sign of anger. They beat their chests in a particular way to produce a sort of hollow tattoo. This is done as a form of display and is most common in the males.

Will a gorilla attack a man?

Gorillas are very peaceful, shy creatures. If they are threatened by people, the leader of the group will put on what looks like a terrifying display, standing upright and beating his chest before dropping on all fours and charging, with ear-shattering roars of what sounds like anger. But this is all in bluff, for the gorilla always stops short before actually attacking. It is widely believed that a gorilla will never attack a man who stands his ground, whereas a person who turns and runs may be chased and mauled. Tribes who live in gorilla country believe that anyone who is injured by a gorilla is a coward, since it shows that he must have tried to run away. Mind you, it can't be easy to stand your ground in face of an over-excited gorilla!

How long do gorillas live?

In the wild, gorillas probably live 20 to 30 years. Females start to breed at about 8 years old, while the males are not fully adult until they are between 10 and 12, by which time they are much larger than the females. In captivity, gorillas have on occasion lived over 40 years.

Are gorillas difficult to keep in captivity?

Until quite recently, very few gorillas ever reached adulthood. This was partly because of wrong feeding, since nobody knew that they were strict vegetarians! But all apes can also easily catch colds and diseases. Nowadays, with better housing and feeding, gorillas are kept successfully in many zoos and breed quite frequently. Most gorillas in captivity are of the lowland race.

Do gorillas walk upright like people?

Gorillas stand upright when beating their chests and may occasionally walk for a few paces in this position. But they normally walk on all fours, resting their weight on the knuckles of their hands.

Are gorillas rare?

The mountain gorillas of central Africa are very rare indeed. In spite of protection, the forests in which they live are still being destroyed and the animals themselves disturbed or even killed. The lowland gorilla of west Africa still exists in fair numbers at present. One of the chief threats to their survival in the past was the widespread hunting of them because of the damage they did to plantations. Adult gorillas have also been killed in order to capture young ones for zoos.

Where are orangutans found?

Orangutans exist in small numbers in the jungles of Borneo and Sumatra in Malaysia. The orangutans from Sumatra are usually slimmer and more lightly coloured than their relatives from Borneo, but both are races of the same animal.

Do orangutans live in groups?

Orangutans are much more solitary than either gorillas or chimpanzees. Normally the adults live singly, or in pairs. A female and her baby stay together until the baby is about four years old. An older child sometimes travels with a mother and her baby or perhaps two or three half-grown orangutans travel together. The really old males live almost entirely alone.

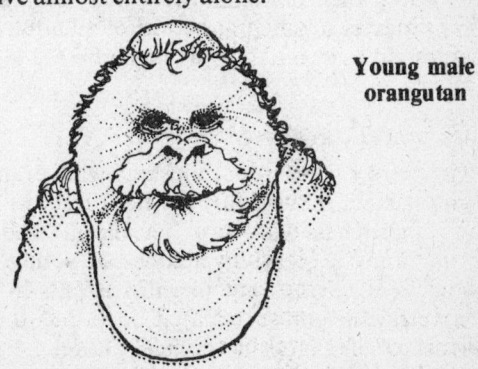

Young male orangutan

How do orangutans live in the wild?

Orangutans live almost entirely in the treetops and rarely come down to the ground. Their long arms and strong hands and feet are marvellously equipped for climbing and travelling in the trees, but on the ground they are slow and awkward. They live on fruits and leaves and spend much of their day travelling through the trees in search of food. At dusk they construct simple nests of twigs and branches high in the trees, from which they do not stir until daybreak.

Are orangutans aggressive?

Wild orangutans are shy, quiet creatures and rarely come face to face with man. Sometimes they show their disapproval at being watched by showering leaves and branches onto the observer, but their aim is not very accurate! Orangutans are immensely strong — in captivity where they have lost their fear of man, the adults, particularly the huge males, can be moody and dangerous.

Just how strong is an orangutan?

An adult male orangutan is usually regarded as being five times as strong as a man. But an adult male gorilla is thought to be ten times as strong!

Are orangutans rare?

There are only a few thousand wild orangutans left. Man has cut down many of the forests where they live and there has also been an illegal trade in young orangutans. Recently a number of young orangutans, which were being kept illegally as pets in Borneo and Sumatra, have been released back into the wild in an effort to safeguard the animals' future.

Where are chimpanzees found?

Chimpanzees are found in forested regions of west and central Africa. In some areas they are also found in more open country where the forest gives way to open bush. They are never found in completely open grassland.

How many species of chimpanzee are there?

Chimpanzees from different parts of Africa differ slightly from each other, but almost all belong to the same species. The only exception is the pygmy chimpanzee or bonobo, from west Africa, which is smaller and more slender than the ordinary chimpanzee and forms a separate species.

Is it true that all chimpanzees look different from each other?

Chimpanzees' faces differ just as much as ours do, and

Chimpanzee

chimpanzees also vary in size and build. This also applies to the gorilla and orangutan. If you look closely at any of the great apes in a zoo you may be able to see these individual differences quite clearly.

Do chimpanzees live in groups or singly?

Chimpanzees live in large, mixed groups of males, females and young. Recent studies of wild chimpanzees show that many groups are composed of females with their young of different ages. Fully adult males either travel with other adult males or accompany female groups. But chimpanzee society is less well organized than a gorilla group and, in time of danger, the group splits up with the animals fleeing in different directions.

What do chimpanzees eat?

Chimpanzees eat a wide variety of fruits and also leaves, shoots and insects. Recently it was discovered that they also eat meat and they have been observed to hunt and kill young baboons and antelope. They also use sticks to poke into ant holes in order to catch the ants which they eat. The use of a tool is very rare in the animal kingdom, and at one time man was thought to be the only animal who was able to use tools.

Do chimpanzees really drink tea?

Only on television and in chimpanzees' tea-parties (which are largely a thing of the past). Chimpanzees in captivity are fed a varied diet including plenty of fruit. They also drink milk and are easily taught to drink from a mug and even to use a spoon for eating. This is because they readily imitate human behaviour.

Are chimpanzees dangerous?

Although not as strong as the larger apes, chimpanzees are at least as powerful as a full-grown man. In captivity the young ones are trained to do a variety of tricks, but the adults are very strong and can be dangerous (the adult males in particular). Wild chimpanzees are very shy and quickly make off into the jungle at the first hint of danger.

Can chimpanzees talk?

Young chimpanzees have been trained to utter a few

words of human speech, but it takes a very long time and a great deal of patience to achieve even a whisper. Despite being intelligent, their natural noise is not strictly a language and chimpanzees cannot 'talk' to each other in the way people can; the variety of sounds and facial expressions they make do succeed in showing their moods and feelings.

Do chimpanzees like dressing up in clothes?

Chimpanzees are very clever at imitating what they see. They are easily taught to put on clothes, drink from a cup and even smoke a cigarette. They seem to take great delight in these antics and often pick up such habits as spitting or begging entirely untaught. Some chimpanzees have also become good at painting!

Are chimpanzees the most intelligent of the great apes?

Chimpanzees, orangutans and gorillas all seem to have equal intelligence. But while the orangutan and the gorilla are shy, quiet animals which often do not show their feelings, the chimpanzee is an excitable, quick-witted clown. Chimpanzees have been observed to use simple tools in the wild, whereas orangutans and gorillas have not. But orangutans in captivity show some remarkable feats of cunning while it is the gorilla which is often thought to be closest to us in its behaviour and intelligence.

Where are gibbons found?

Gibbons live in forested regions of south-east Asia. There are several different species. Unlike most of the other apes and monkeys, gibbons do not live in large groups but in family units. Each group consists of a male, a female and young of different ages. In this respect they closely resemble the usual human family.

Gibbon

Which of the great apes is closest to man?

The gorilla has the largest brain size of the three great apes, but it still has only one-third the capacity of man's. On the other hand, tests have shown that the blood of the chimpanzee is the most similar to ours. In fact, modern man is not directly descended from any of the great apes. We evolved along another branch of the evolutionary 'tree'.

What is a Barbary ape?

The Barbary ape is a species of monkey found in north Africa. It is called 'ape' because it has no visible tail. Barbary apes are also found living on the Rock of

Gibraltar, the only place in Europe where monkeys are found. No one knows if they have always lived there, or if they were brought there by man. There is a saying that if ever the Barbary apes die out on Gibraltar, the British will lose possession of it. This nearly happened during World War Two, when there were only five of them left. Some more were hastily obtained from north Africa, just in case the story was true!

Which is the largest of the monkeys?

The mandrill of west Africa is among the largest of all the monkeys and its close relative the drill is only slightly smaller. An adult male mandrill is almost the size of a chimpanzee. These are the monkeys with the brilliantly coloured blue and red faces and matching bottoms, which are a favourite attraction in zoos.

Are baboons the same as monkeys?

Baboons are a family of monkeys which have become adapted to a life spent living more on the ground than in trees. Baboons travel in large troops, seeking safety in numbers from enemies such as leopards. Each troop includes several adult males which act as guards to the females and young. Each animal in the troop has its own rank.

Baboons sleep in trees or high up on rock faces, but move and get their food on the ground. Their faces are more dog-like than those of other monkeys.

What do monkeys eat?

Most species of monkey eat fruits, shoots and a variety of insects, grains and seeds. Some, such as the colobus monkeys of Africa and the langurs of Asia eat only leaves and have stomachs which are specially designed to cope with such a tough diet.

White nosed Mangabey monkey (found in east coast Africa)

Which are the smallest monkeys?

The smallest of the monkeys are the tiny marmosets and tamarins, little South American species which could easily sit in the palm of your hand.

How many young do apes and monkeys have?

All the apes and nearly all the monkeys give birth to only one young at a time. All three kinds of great ape have been recorded as giving birth to twins in captivity, but this is very rare. In the wild, it is unlikely that both young would survive. However, the tiny marmosets of South America quite commonly give birth to twins.

They are also unusual in that it is the father, not the mother, that carries the babies for much of the time!

What are lemurs?

Lemurs are a very primitive group of monkeys, found only in Madagascar. Altogether there are 19 species, but they are very different in shape and size. The indris is almost as large as a chimpanzee, but unlike the chimp it has long hind legs and a slim body. There are several medium-sized lemurs, one of which — the ring-tailed lemur — is frequently seen in captivity. The mouse lemurs are tiny, mouse-sized animals, as their name suggests.

Are lemurs rare?

Lemurs are in great danger of extinction, because their forests are being drastically reduced. One species, the aye-aye, is one of the rarest mammals in the world, and many of the other species are also found only in very small numxers.

What are the main enemies of monkeys and apes?

Monkeys are preyed upon by a variety of creatures, depending on the country in which they live. Big cats, such as leopards, jaguars and tigers, all eat monkeys when they can catch them. Snakes and eagles are also monkey-eaters in some areas. For many species the chief enemy is man, who shoots them for their skins or for food, or traps them alive to sell to animal dealers.

The three great apes have very few natural enemies at all. The main threat to their continued survival is man, who cuts down the forests in which these animals are found and disturbs the animals further by capturing the young for sale abroad.

MORE CHILDREN'S **LOOK-IN** BOOKS

Second Runaround Quiz Book 60p
Elizabeth Bland

Stewpot's Fun Book 65p
Denis Gifford

Stewpot's Travel Fun Book 60p
George & Cornelia Kay

Fun With Words 60p
Eric Linden

Warriors of the West 60p
Robin May

Clifton House Mystery 60p
Daniel Farson

These books can be obtained from your bookshops or directly from:

ITV Books
Small Orders Department
P O Box 29
Douglas
Isle of Man

Cheques/postal orders (including 10p for postage and packing) should be made payable to: Book Service By Post.